HUMAN BEING IN DEPTH

Sri Garib Das Oriental Series No. 194

HUMAN BEING IN DEPTH

A Scientific Approach to Religion

by

SWAMI RANGANATHANANDA

with Foreword by Janet A. Walker

Edited by Elva Linnéa Nelson

SRI SATGURU PUBLICATIONS
A DIVISION OF
INDIAN BOOKS CENTRE
DELHI-INDIA

Published by:
Sri Satguru Publications
Indological and Oriental Publishers
A Division of
Indian Books Centre
40/5, Shakti Nagar,
Delhi-110007
(INDIA)

The Publication of this Book in India is made by Permission of State University of New York Press.

First Indian Edition: Delhi, 1995

ISBN 81-7030-473-3

Printed at : Mehra Offset Press, New Delhi.

PRINTED IN INDIA

Contents

Preface

The main theme of this book, *Human Being in Depth: A Scientific Approach to Religion,* is that, although there may have been conflicts between science and religion in the Western experience, there has been only harmony between these two disciplines in the over four thousand yearlong historical experience of India. India's approach to religion is rational and experiential; it encourages questioning and inquiry like any of the physical sciences. It follows that with such an approach there were no persecutions of scientists, or even of atheists or agnostics.

In the course of this book, I have referred to the views of several modern Western scientists and Eastern philosophers and mystics in support of the main theme. Since writing the book, many more books by Western scientists and thinkers have appeared, strengthening this conviction. In the introduction to his book: *The Meeting of the Ways: Explorations in East / West Psychology,* John Welwood says:

> The present encounter of the experiential, holistic, and enlightenment-oriented traditions of the East with the precision, clarity, skepticism, and independence of Western methods could lead to a new kind of psychology that transcends cultural limitations and opens up what Abraham Maslow referred to as 'the farther reaches of human nature.' Such a new form of East / West psychology, as represented embryonically in the articles assembled here, is only in its infancy but it does not appear to be just a passing cultural fancy. May this book contribute to its further growth. [p.xv–xvi]

This book, *Human Being in Depth,* emphasizes the need for the modern man or woman to cultivate a spiritual temper along with a scientific temper and to make the two energy streams of physical science and the science of spirituality flow together for the total welfare and fulfillment of humanity.

If this book helps, even a little, to stimulate the readers toward this conviction and effort, the author will feel amply rewarded.

I am thankful to Dr. Kurt F. Leidecker, Professor Emeritus of philosophy, Mary Washington College, for his early and continued encouragement. To Dr. Janet A. Walker, Associate Professor of comparative literature, Rutgers University for her expertise and gracious interest in writing the foreword, and to Elva Linnéa Nelson for her loving labor in editing and preparing the book for publication.

Swami Ranganathananda
Boston, Mass.
May 1989

Acknowledgments

Grateful acknowledgment is made to the following for permission to reprint previously published material:

Harper and Row Publishers, Inc. from *Physics and Philosophy,* vol. 19 of World Perspectives, by Werner Heisenberg; Planned and edited by Ruth Nanda Anshen. Copyright 1958 by Werner Heisenberg.

From *The Secret Life of Plants,* by Peter Tompkins. Copyright 1973 by Peter Tompkins and Christopher Bird and Penguin Books Ltd., London.

From *The Phenomenon of Man,* by Pierre Teilhard de Chardin. Copyright 1955 by Editions de Seuil. English translation copyright 1959 by William Collins Sons and Co., Ltd, London, and Harper and Row Publishers, Inc., of New York.

From *Consciousness: Brain, States of Awareness, and Alternate Realities.* Copyright 1979 by Daniel Goleman and Richard J. Davidson.

The University of Chicago Press. From *Evolution after Darwin,* ed. by Sol Tax and Charles Callender. Copyright 1960 by University of Chicago.

George Allen & Unwin, England. From *Impact of Science on Society,* by Bertrand Russell. Copyright, 1952.

Oxford University Press, England. From *The Thirteen Principal Upanishads,* by Robert Ernest Hume, 2 ed., 1931. Copyright 1931 by Oxford University Press.

From *Eastern Religions and Western Thought,* by Sarvepali Radhakrishnan. 2 ed., Copyright 1940 by Oxford University Press.

Cambridge University Press, New York. From *The New Background of Science,* by Sir James Jeans. Copyright 1947 by Cambridge University Press.

From Erwin Schroedinger's *What is Life.* Copyright 1944 by Cambridge University Press.

From *Philosophy of Physical Science,* by Sir Arthur Eddington. Copyright 1939 by Cambridge University Press.

From *Space, Time, and Gravitation,* by Sir Arthur Eddington. Copyright 1966 by Cambridge University Press.

From *The Nature of the Physical World,* by Sir Arthur Eddington. Copyright 1928 by Cambridge University Press.

From *Man on His Nature,* by Sir Charles Sherrington. Pelican ed., 1935. Copyright 1935 by Cambridge University Press.

Yale University Press. From *The Meaning of Evolution,* by George Gaylord Simpson. Copyright 1964 by Yale University Press.

Routledge and Kegan Paul. From *Dialogues with Scientists and Sages,* ed. by Renée Weber. Copyright 1986 by Renée Weber.

From *Quantam Implications,* ed. by Hiley and Peat. Copyright 1987 by Routledge and Kegan Paul.

Lyle Stuart, Inc. From *Out of My Later Years,* by Albert Einstein. Citadel Press, copyright 1974. Copyright 1950 by Philosophical Library.

W. H. Freeman and Co. From *The Nature of Human Consciousness,* ed. by Robert E. Ornstein. Copyright 1973 by Robert Evans Ornstein.

Curtis Brown Ltd. From *The Universe and Dr. Einstein,* by Lincoln Barnett. Published by William Morrow and Co. Copyright 1948 by Lincoln Barnett.

Gerald Duckworth and Co. Ltd. From *The Living Brain,* by William Grey Walter. Copyright 1963 by Gerald Duckworth and Co., Ltd.

Holt, Rinehart and Winston. From *Introduction to Science,* by J. Arthur Thompson. Home University Library ed. 1934. Copyright 1911 by Henry Holt and Co.

Shambala Publications, Inc. From *Quantum Questions* by Ken Wilber. New Science Library, Copyright 1984 by Ken Wilber.

From *The Tao of Physics* by Fritjof Capra. Shambala Publications, USA and Wildwood House, U.K., 1974. Copyright 1975 by Fritjof Capra.

Random House. From *The Meeting of the Ways: Explorations* in East/West Psychology, ed. by John Welwood. Copyright by Schocken Books, Inc. 1979.

Addison-Wesley. From *An Outline of Animal Development* by Richard Davenport. Copyright 1979 by Addison-Wesley.

From *The Highest State of Consciousness,* reproduced by kind permission of the author, John White. Published by Doubleday and Co., Inc., and Anchor Books. Copyright 1972 by John White.

For material used in their publications Advaita Ashrama, Calcutta; and Bharatiya Vidya Bhavan, Bombay, India.

Foreword

A number of books have appeared since the 1970s that attempt an exposition of the similarities between the disciplines of science and religion. Their goal is to argue for the advantages, or the necessities, of a rapprochement between them. However, these are by professional scientists and philosophers, or by generalist writers on science. The present book by Swami Ranganathananda is the first one on this topic by a spiritual teacher. It combines a depth of conviction, stemming from his calling as a teacher, with an understanding of the scientific mode of thinking.

Swami Ranganathananda commences from the acute sense that modern Westerners, facing ecological and political crises of the outer world as well as psychological and spiritual crises of the inner world, are much in need of a path of practical spiritual evolution. Since the mid-nineteenth century, when mechanistic science all but replaced traditional religion as a mode of thinking about the world, westerners have had a tendency to view religion as unscientific and therefore useless as a guide to action. Yet mechanistic science offers nothing of substance to the soul. Swami Ranganathananda argues that the post-Newtonian science of the twentieth century, with its sense of the mystery of the inner world and its interest in viewing human nature in depth, provides the possibility for the acceptance of the idea of a "science of the facts pertaining to our inner spiritual world."

This kind of science is what Vedanta, a perennial philosophy first manifested in the *Upanishads*, and expounded more recently, in the late nineteenth century, by Swami Vivekananda, has to offer the West. In three closely interconnected essays, Swami Ranganathananda explains how Vedanta, congruent with modern scientific thinking, in its desire to understand nature, even human nature, through dispassionate inquiry, provides a discipline that leads to the understanding of human nature in its deepest reaches. In chapter 1 he gives an overview of the ways in which Vedanta is similar in its "spirit, temper, and objectives" to twentieth-century science. Vedanta shares with modern science an emphasis on the spirit of critical discrimination and inner detachment, and a faith in the human capacity to unravel the mystery of the world. But it goes beyond physical science in its ability to chart a systematic path of human evolution – a path that sets as its goal the solution of the "mystery of the universe" through the "solution of the mystery disclosed within our own nature."

Chapter 2 focuses on the nature of truth in Vedanta, and the attitude of faith needed to pursue it. Faith in Vedanta is not a blind belief in a dogma or a divinity but a positive conviction, which is found also in modern science, that there is truth hidden somewhere in the recesses of life. The truth that one experiences in Vedanta is "pure Consciousness." Chapter 3 centers on that truth. Swami Ranganathananda describes the Upanishadic Atman-Brahman as a "consciousness-field" similar to the unified field of modern science. He posits human life as not merely an "external journey in space and time" but also as an "inner spiritual journey" in which one penetrates to the truth of spiritual energy. That there is an "immortal Self behind the mortal mind-body complex" is a "spiritual fact" capable of being realized by every human being.

Swami Ranganathananda has built a bridge that joins Western science with Vedantic spirituality. He was born in 1908 in a village near Trichur, in Kerala. Moved deeply as a teenager by the teachings of Swami Vivekananda as well as the teachings of the latter's master, Sri Ramakrishna, he joined the Ramakrishna Order in 1926. After initiation as a-monk in 1933, on the anniversay of Swami Vivekananda's birth, he served the Order in Mysore, Bangalore, Rangoon, Karachi, Delhi, and Calcutta. He is the founder and the present head of the Ramakrishna Math in Hyderabad. In 1986, he was the first recipient of the Indira Gandhi Award for National Integration and in 1988 he was elected one of the vice-presidents of the Ramakrishna Order.

Since his residence in Bangalore in the 1930s, Swami Ranganathananda has been a popular teacher and lecturer on Indian spiritual culture. By the mid-1950s he was known within India as an authority on practical Vedanta. He continues to lecture widely in India, and since the 1960s he has made nearly annual lecture tours to Western Europe, the United States, Australia, and Singapore. He has also lectured in Iran and in the Soviet Union. As a lecturer he succeeds in discussing the highest spiritual ideas with the utter clarity and concreteness of one who has attained a high level of spiritual realization. When he lectures, he gives the effect of a teacher speaking with intense concern for the spiritual welfare and growth of each individual present. I believe that readers will find this concern transmitted in the present manuscript.

It was during one of his first lecture tours to the United States, in 1969, that I heard Swami Ranganathananda speak for the first time; I was a graduate student at Harvard. I felt and continue to feel privileged to have had the chance to not only hear him but also to speak with him several more times since then; he has been an undeniable influence on my personal "inner spiritual journey."

One of the important messages of this book is that "the spiritual growth of humanity is a fact. And the more we know the science and technique of this growth, the better for us and society." Swami Ranganathananda, in the following pages, points out an elevated goal for humanity. He also suggests how one might go about attaining it, interspersing his own remarks with many quotations from Vedantic thinkers and Western scientists and philosophers. Above all, he inspires the reader to pursue this goal by presenting the spiritual path as a "high adventure of the spirit, a life endeavor to realize and grasp the hidden meaning of existence." It is this message that is supported by Vedanta.

JANET A. WALKER
Rutgers University

NOTE:

Wherever there is Sanskrit in the text, it is accompanied by an English translation. We have, however, provided a brief glossary of Sanskrit words at the end. The commentaries of Shankaracharya have been, with one exception, translated by Swami Ranganathananda.

Human Being In Depth: Science and Religion

Even while confronted by, and engaged in tackling, the mystery of the external universe, modern science has become impressed with a deeper mystery, the mystery of our inner being, the challenge of the world within.

We, in the modern world, are like that great statue, The Thinker, by Rodin, pondering on the results of our technology and science, focusing our attention on many divergent areas such as nuclear reactors, ecological disasters, genetic engineering, and drug addiction. Modern social and environmental problems such as these may be responsible in the advanced countries of the world for a certain growing distrust of science and technology; but science, with its passion for truth and mindful of human welfare, will always remain one of our noblest pursuits.

Is our age devoid of another truth – the truth of religion? Religion and philosophy, as embodied in the tradition of India going back to the *Upanishads*, her first philosophical treatises, are but the continuation of the scientific search for truth at the sense-data level raised to the higher aesthetic, spiritual and value systems levels of experience. Can there be a rapprochement between these two great areas of human concern?

Science and religion are becoming evermore important in the modern age. They are the two great disciplines which, in the light of Indian wisdom, can, when relied on separately, be counterproductive in the long run, but when combined harmoniously, become an all-round expression of human genius and make for total fulfillment. Unfortunately, the relationships between the two during the last few centuries, be it in the West or wherever Western influence has been felt, has not been a very happy one.

In the twentieth century, however, a new approach is becoming evident with representative thinkers among scientists and religious people beginning to discern an interrelation between them. They are slowly veering round to the point of view that science and religion can, indeed, embrace each other without detriment to the cause for which each stands and works for the good of humanity. It is being realized more and more by both factions that there are elements in science that religion can adopt in order to fortify itself, and elements in religion that can deepen and strengthen science.

Our purpose is to touch upon some of the sources of the traditional discord between science and religion and the significance of the points of contact between them, and to discuss the methods and results of both disciplines against the background and in the light of the unity and totality of human knowledge, together with a synthetic and synoptic approach by the philosophical tradition of India.

RELATIONSHIP OF SCIENCE AND RELIGION: A NEW APPROACH

When we study science closely in the way the great scientists have applied themselves to its pursuit, we find two aspects to this discipline. The first is pure science, that is, science that tries earnestly to understand nature through dispassionate inquiry; and the second is applied science, in which truth discovered by pure science is translated, as it were, into technical inventions for the enhancement and enrichment of human life.

The result is the great saga of modern discoveries and inventions resulting in our worldwide technological civilization: our extraordinary age of nuclear science, space travel, and genetic codes. What is the nature of that movement of thought that produced these remarkable results? What is the special feature of modern scientific thought that has rendered thought so explosive and revolutionary? An answer to these questions will help us to reassess the role of the other great human disciplines of our age, such as religion, ethics, politics, art, and economics.

From a historical perspective, what distinguishes our modern world from other periods of history is the stress on science. Science is in the forefront as an architect of our world. So by modern thought is meant scientific thought. The aim of science is to study nature and human experience objectively as Karl Pearson stated in his *Grammar of Science*:

> The classification of facts, the recognition of their sequence and relative significance, is the function of science, and the habit of forming a judgment upon these facts unbiased by personal feeling is characteristic of what may be termed the scientific frame of mind.[1]

The sum total of achievements in the theoretical and practical fields in the various departments of scientific inquiry in physics and chemistry, mathematics and astronomy, biology, and psychology, as well as in their various subsidiary branches, constitute an impressive record of human achievement. Compared with it, the achievements of the past in the same fields pale into insignificance. Science, objective, impersonal, and verifiable is not confined to any particular body of facts. In the words of one of the great biologists, J. Arthur Thomson, in his *Introduction to Science*:

> Science is not wrapped up with any particular body of facts; it is characterised as an intellectual attitude. It is not tied down to any particular methods of inquiry; it is simply sincere critical thought, which admits conclusions only when these are based on evidence. We may get a good

> lesson in scientific method from a businessman meeting some new practical problem, from a lawyer sifting evidence, or from a statesman framing a constructive bill.[2]

Objectivity and precision, both as to thought and its verbal formulation, are two important characteristics of the scientific method. Any study possessing these characteristics will be scientific, whatever the field of study. Science as such is, therefore, not linked to any particular order of facts, but is an investigation applied to various classes of phenomena. Starting with the study of the separate fields of natural phenomena, these branches tend, in their advanced development, to transcend their boundaries and to merge into one overriding scientific search, the search for the meaning of total experience. In this expansive context, the idea of a science of religion, that is, the science of the facts, pertaining to our inner spiritual world as upheld in ancient Indian thought and expounded in the last century by Swami Vivekananda, likewise becomes a scientific study of far-reaching significance.

The driving force behind the unique modern scientific achievements is the spirit of free inquiry. The mind that questions and questions with a serious intent and purpose, that tests and verifies the answer it gets, has a dynamic quality about it that enables it to forge ahead in the world of thought and phenomena to be studied. The freedom to question can unsettle every untested dogma and comfortable belief, whether scientific or religious. In the field of religion, it has been doing away with magic and superstition, all of which have been wrongly associated with it and thus were contributing to the vulgarization of this great discipline. Science is indeed verifiable knowledge following its own methodology.

The explosive character of modern scientific thought by its impact of a rapid succession of verified knowledge on an intractable fund of dogmas, assumptions, beliefs, magical practices, miracles and superstitions, all of which had gone untested, did not go unnoticed. The exponents of those vagaries of religion in the West sought to stifle scientific inquiry, first at its inception and then at every stage of its progress. But the walls of the *bastille* of ignorance and prejudice fell one by one before the onrushing waves of scientific inquiry and illumination, illustrating the great saying of the *Mundaka Upanishad* [III.1.6]: *Satyameva jayate, nanrtam*— "Truth alone triumphs, not untruth."

Unfortunately the forces of prejudice and blind belief against science and its spirit of inquiry came from religion, and that reason, which is the life breath of science, was viewed as the death knell of religion. By the end of the last century, science had acquired its high prestige and authority, while religion was being discredited, first as a grievous error, and later as a harmless illusion.

The end of the nineteenth century saw for many the eclipse of religion in the West. Nevertheless, there was an uneasy feeling in the hearts of many thinkers that something of deep value to humanity and to civilization had been cast away. Consequently they attempted a reassessment of the meaning and scope of religion with a view to bringing it into accord with the spirit and temper of science. In this great task of reconstructing the mental life of modern humanity by bridging the gulf between faith and reason on the basis of a unified view of human nature and a more adequate conception of spiritual life, the contribution of Indian thought is unique and lasting.

Tracing the recurring conflicts of science and religion in the West to the absence of a broad rational and experiential approach, Swami Vivekananda said, after attending the Parliament of Religions in Chicago in 1893, and after having met some of the foremost thinkers in the West:

> We all know the theories of the cosmos according to the modern astronomers and physicists, and at the same time we all know how woefully they undermine the theology of Europe; how these scientific discoveries that are made act as a bomb thrown at its stronghold; and we know how theologians have in all times attempted to put down these researches.[3]

When religion refuses to invoke the aid of reason, it weakens itself. Alluding to this in the course of a lecture on *Reason and Religion*, delivered in England in 1896, which we still find timely, Swami Vivekananda said:

> The foundations have been all undermined, and modern man, whatever he may say in public, knows in the privacy of his heart that he can no more "believe." Believing certain things because an organised body of priests tells him to believe, believing because it is written in certain books, believing because his people like him to believe, the modern man knows to be impossible for him. There are, of course, a number of people who seem to acquiesce in the so-called popular faith, but we also know for certain that they do not think. Their idea of belief may be better translated as "not-thinking-carelessness!"[4]

And, pleading for the application of reason in the field of religion, he continued:

> . . . Is religion to justify itself by the discoveries of reason through which every other science justifies itself? Are the same methods of investigation, which we apply to science and knowledge outside, to be applied to the science of religion? In my opinion, this must be so; and I am also of opinion that the sooner it is done the better. If a religion is destroyed

> by such investigations, it was then all the time useless, unworthy, superstition; and the sooner it goes the better. I am thoroughly convinced that its destruction would be the best thing that could happen. All that is dross will be taken off, no doubt, but the essential parts of religion will emerge triumphant out of this investigation. Not only will it be made scientific—as scientific, at least, as any of the conclusions of physics or chemistry—but it will have greater strength, because physics or chemistry has no internal mandate to vouch for its truth which religion has.[5]

A study of the *Upanishads* reveals that the subject of religion was approached in ancient India in an impersonal and dispassionate manner. The aim of the study was neither to hug pleasing fancies and illusions nor to idolize tribal passions and prejudices but to get at the truth.

While lecturing throughout the Western world, as well as in India, Swami Vivekananda expounded this scientific approach as upheld in Indian thought. In his lecture on *Religion and Science*, he says:

> Experience is the only source of knowledge. In the world, religion is the only science where there is no surety, because it is not taught as a science of experience. This should not be. There is always, however, a small group of men who teach religion from experience. They are called mystics, and these mystics in every religion speak the same tongue and teach the same truth. This is the real science of religion. As mathematics in every part of the world does not differ, so the mystics do not differ. They are all similarly constituted and similarly situated. Their experience is the same; and this becomes law. . . .
>
> Religion deals with the truths of the metaphysical world, just as chemistry and the other natural sciences deal with the truths of the physical world. The book one must read to learn chemistry is the book of nature. The book from which to learn religion is your own mind and heart. The sage is often ignorant of physical science, because he reads the wrong book—the book within; and the scientist is too often ignorant of religion, because he, too, reads the wrong book—the book without.[6]

The Indian thinkers discovered in their investigations that there are two fields in which people live and function: one, the external world, the other, the internal one. The study of only one does not exhaust the whole range of experience, nor will the study of the one from the standpoint of the other lead to satisfactory results. But the study of one *in the light of the conclusions from the study of the other* is helpful and relevant.

Referring to this approach in the course of a lecture on *Cosmology*, Swami Vivekananda has this comment:

> There are two worlds: the microcosm and the macrocosm, the internal and the external. We get truth from both of these by means of experi-

> ence. The truth gathered from internal experience is psychology, metaphysics, and religion; from external experience, the physical sciences. Now, a perfect truth should be in harmony with experiences in both these worlds. The microcosm must bear testimony to the macrocosm, and the macrocosm to the microcosm; physical truth must have its counter part in the internal world, and the internal world must have its verification outside.[7]

Similarly, the sages and thinkers of ancient India said: Here is the physical life of men and women, and here is the physical universe that environs them. Let us study both in a scientific spirit. But let us also study human being-in-depth, its nature as revealed by consciousness, by thoughts, by emotions, by ego, and by the sense of selfhood. These, too, constitute a vast group of phenomena that needs to be investigated. Every advance in this field is bound to advance our knowledge about the mystery of the external world. For, to quote mathematics-astronomer Sir Arthur Eddington from his *Philosophy of Physical Science*:

> We have discovered that it is actually an aid in the search for knowledge to understand the nature of the knowledge which we seek.[8]

THE *UPANISHADS* AND THE SPIRIT OF CRITICAL INQUIRY IN INDIA

Ever since the time of the *Upanishads,* which goes back long before the Christian era, India has tenaciously held to a view of religion that makes it a high adventure of the spirit, a life endeavor to realize and grasp the hidden meaning of existence. Faith in India did not mean a cozy belief in which to find comfort, but a torch by which to set the soul on fire with a longing for spiritual realization. In the absence of this longing and struggle, the belief of the faithful does not differ from the unbelief of the faithless.

Belief with most people is simply another name for mental laziness. Religious earnestness with people of this class means, especially when organized under a militant church or a theocratic state, either the pursuit of aggressive proselytism or *jehads* and crusades. They cannot understand the meaning of that earnestness that proceeds from an inner spiritual hunger. No dogma or creed or frenzied acts can satisfy this hunger of a religious heart. Its only bread is spiritual realization. Religion is a matter of inner experience, a getting in touch with spiritual facts of the supersensory levels of experience, not a matter of belief, dogma or conformity.

Because of the strength of the spirit of the *Upanishads,* no all-powerful church, therefore, arose in India to organize the faithful on the basis of dogma and creed, claiming divine authority for its opinions and judgments. No such authority could thrive where religion was expounded as a quest and not a conformity. A spiritual view of religion, as different from a creedal or dogmatic one, compels the religious not only to cultivate a spirit of toleration, questioning, and inquiry within their own sphere of religion, but to foster it also in every department of life.

Bhagavad Gita [VI. 44.] declares that a spirit of inquiry into the meaning of religion takes an aspirant beyond the authority of the words of the scripture and the mandate of tradition. One becomes an experimenter, instead of remaining a mere believer. Indian religious thought emphasizes experiment (*sadhana*) as the dynamic element in religion. It counsels recourse to inquiry (*jijnasa*) for the formulation of its views, be it inquiry into the nature of Brahman, that is, God as the One Self of all, or inquiry into *dharma*, social ethics, and personal morality.

This sublime attitude in religion and thought is the fruit of the unified view of the mental life of humanity that India learned from her *Upanishads*, which she then has assimilated into her mind and mood by a universal acceptance of all forms of faith; she shows due regard for all knowledge, whether sacred or secular.

Science in the modern age has lengthened our intellectual tether, but this has only helped to bring into sharper focus the mystery of the unknown and the significance of the higher knowledge or wisdom (*paravidya*) of which the *Upanishads* speak. In the words of J. Arthur Thompson: "At the end of his intellectual tether, man has never ceased to become religious."[9]

It is no wonder, therefore, that in the post-WWII period, several scientists have been forced to overstep the limits of their particular branches of science and write books of a philosophical nature, and thus tackle the problem of the unknown at close range in a mood of humility and reverence, illustrating the dictum of Indian wisdom: *vidya dadati vinayam*—knowledge bestows humility—and the saying of Samuel Coleridge quoted by J. Arthur Thompson: "All knowledge begins and ends with wonder; but the first wonder is the child of ignorance; the second wonder is the parent of adoration."[10]

Dogmatism and overconfidence, which stifle the spirit of free inquiry, are as much enemies of true science as of true religion. Should there be only a few scientists who would, by taking a narrow view of the scope and function of science, prefer to cry a halt to advancing knowledge, that would imply a danger to science and unified knowledge, just as it had spelled danger to religion before. A greater devotion to the spirit of free inquiry and a broader conception of the aim and temper of science is our only safeguard against such a pitfall.

If the nineteenth century was the century of conflict and division, the twentieth century bids fair to become the century of reconciliation and union as a result of a sincere effort on the part of both science and religion to reassess itself and understand one another. The humility of twentieth-century science, for the most part, presents a sharp and welcome contrast to the attitude of its nineteenth century counterpart. It has realized that the spirit of free inquiry on which it has thrived may find expression in fields beyond its own narrow departments, and that it is this spirit, unbiased by personal attachments and aversions, that makes a study scientific, not the mere subject matter of that study.

This wider view of science as a discipline and a temper enables us to class as scientific the study of facts of the inner world, which religion has set itself to inquire.

This has been India's approach to religion. It was the absence of this approach that has made religion in the West less and less equipped to meet the challenge of advancing knowledge.

LIMITATIONS OF PHYSICAL SCIENCE

When we go deeper into the nature and scope of physical science, its limitations become apparent. To illustrate: two branches of science, physics inclusive of astronomy, and biology inclusive of behavioristic psychology, have given us a vast body of knowledge regarding the nature of the universe and of our human nature. Up to the end of the nineteenth century and even into the early twentieth century through the 1920s, there were those like Joseph Needham and his book, *Man a Machine*, who proclaimed unabashedly that materialism and mechanism reigned supreme in the universe.

In the nineteenth century, knowledge of the physical world was not thorough enough, and scientists were looking, as it were, only at the surface of things. But, along with the discovery of radioactivity, atomic fission and the like, there came the realization that severe limitations are placed on our knowledge regarding the nature of the external world. Science admits today that it deals only with the appearance of things and not with the reality behind these appearances. Some of the greatest of modern physicists tell us that what science has revealed of the world around us is only the outer aspect of things. Behind this observable universe, there is an unobservable, inferential universe, and there is the observer who cannot be left out. And all science is a continuing search from the observable to the unobservable.

This is a great confession as to the limitations of science and its methods. Science is dealing with phenomena revealed by the senses or by apparatuses helpful to the senses. But these senses reveal very little, and what they do reveal only tells us that there are realities behind the sense world that determine and control it. Physics mainly restricts itself to the understanding of the observable part of the universe and to harnessing energies. A similar situation is obtained in biology.

In the last century, it was absolutely certain about its pronouncements. By studying the different aspects of the phenomena of life, it arrived at the theory of evolution. From it some biologists drew certain conclusions influenced by the mechanistic materialism of contemporary physics, and thus were directly led to a form of materialism that equated people and animals, and likened both to a machine.

Scientists now tell us that these were not happy titles that Charles Darwin chose for his famous books: *The Origin of Species* and *The Descent of Man*. Sir Julian Huxley has suggested that they could have been more appropriately titled: *The Evolution of Organisms* and *The Ascent of Man*.[11] But, then, these books appeared at a time when a fierce controversy was going on between science and the entrenched Christian dogma of supernaturalism, which speaks of humanity as a special creation of an extracosmic God.

Physics with its thoroughgoing materialism and mechanistic determinism, and biology with its newly discovered evolutionary theory, being dominated by the general materialistic outlook of science, helped to shatter the faith of the nineteenth century in religion and spiritual values, which now became stigmatized in the West as anti-science.

The limitations of physical science, having been admitted by many modern scientists, proceed from the adjective *physical*; but science itself is not limited similarly. Reality may be studied, but not exhausted, by the physical sciences, whose limitations are due to their dependence entirely on sense-data. These limitations have been pointed out by Sir Arthur Eddington:

> Let us suppose that an ichthyologist is exploring the life of the ocean. He casts a net into the water and brings up a fishy assortment. Surveying his catch, he proceeds, in the usual manner of a scientist, to systematise what it reveals. He arrives at two generalisations:
>
> 1. No sea-creature is less than two inches long.
> 2. All sea-creatures have gills.
>
> These are both true of his catch, and he assumes tentatively that they will remain true however often he repeats it. His generalization is perfectly true of the class of creatures he is talking about—a selected class perhaps, but he would not be interested in making generalisations about any other class.[12]

Earlier, Eddington said:

> I am not among those who think that, in the search for truth, all aspects of human experience are to be ignored, save those which are followed up in physical science. But I find no disharmony between a philosohy which embraces the wider significance of human experience and the specialised philosophy of physical science, even though the latter relates to a system of thought of recent growth whose stability is yet to be tested.[13]

After terming materialism an intruder in his book *Methods and Results*, Thomas Huxley, the collaborator of Darwin, repudiates materialism as a philosophy of life:

> . . . If we find that the ascertainment of the order of nature, is facilitated by using one terminology or set of symbols, rather than another, it is our clear duty to use the former; and no harm can accrue, so long as we bear in mind that we are dealing with terms and symbols. . . .
>
> But the man of science who, forgetting the limits of philosophical inquiry, slides from these formulae and symbols into what is commonly understood by materialism, seems to me to place himself on a level with the mathematician who should mistake the x's and y's with which he works his problems for real entities—and with this further disadvantage, as compared with the mathematician, that the blunders of the latter are of no practical consequence, while the errors of systematic materialism may paralyse the energies and destroy the beauty of life.[14]

Fortunately, a new breeze seems to be blowing in the scientific world. In contrast to materialism and the mechanistic approach of earlier scientists there is now a diametrically opposite point of view as set forth by Willis Harman: "Consciousness is not the end-product of material evolution; rather, consciousness was here first!" and, "The idea of matter emerging out of consciousness seems quite foreign to the Western mind . . ."[15]

Now there are concepts like Rupert Sheldrake's morphic resonance and in cosmology the ten dimensional universe. Leaps of the imagination that would have staggered even the scientists of the Nineteenth century.

THE MYSTERY OF THE UNIVERSE AND THE MYSTERY OF HUMAN NATURE

The universe was a mystery to primitive humanity; it has not ceased to be so for civilized humanity even in this twentieth century. We find scientists like the late Sir James Jeans writing books on the scientific view of the universe with such titles as *The Mysterious Universe*. And in the microuniverse of nature, mysterious still at the present time, we find scientists like Rupert Sheldrake putting forth a hypothesis of formative causation. If, after all these marvelous scientific discoveries, scientists still treat nature as profoundly mysterious and if, in spite of all the vast knowledge that has been gained, they feel that they have only scratched the surface of nature and are still far from the heart of the problem of the universe, we have to pause and ask the question as framed by Shankaracharya: *Tatah kim tatah kim?*—"what next what next?"

Says Sir James Jeans in his *The New Background of Science*:

> Physical science set out to study a world of matter and radiation, and finds that it cannot describe or picture the nature of either, even to itself. Photons, electrons, and protons have become about as meaningless to the physicist as x, y, and z are to a child on its first day of learning algebra. The most we hope for at the moment is to discover ways of manipulating x, y, z without knowing what they are, with the result that the advance of knowledge is at present reduced to what Einstein has described as extracting one incomprehensible from another incomprehensible.[16]

Even while confronted by, and engaged in tackling, the mystery of the external universe, modern science has become impressed with a deeper mystery, the mystery of human nature, the challenge of its inner world. The physical dimension poses no challenge to a science that has achieved revolutionary advances in anatomy and physiology, neurology and microbiology, medicine and behavioristic psychology. But these disciplines point to a mysterious depth in our being, which reveals a new dimension to nature herself, namely, her *within*, over and above her *without*. Earlier scientists like Alexis Carrel in his *Man the Unknown*, and in recent years neurologists like Grey Walter and Wilder Penfield in his mind-brain studies published as *The Mystery of the Mind* have turned their attention to this great mystery.

We in our human nature reveal dimensions that cannot be reduced to the merely physical, the merely material. These latter are our "notself" aspects that enter into the constitution of our body, which obviously is just a speck of duct in that vast world of the not-self. But there is in us also something transcendant that cannot be so reduced. It is the "Self." " . . . the nature of the Self is Pure Consciousness."[17] *That* is our primary inalienable aspect. And if science is to progress further, it must choose for investigation this field of the mystery within us that towers over science's former concern, the mystery of the external universe.

This is a vast field of study—the field of humanity's self-awareness, the field of consciousness, ego, humanity being *subject*, not *object*. Science will find here a vaster, more fascinating and rewarding research than in external nature. Already scientists in the West are slowly turning their attention to this great mystery, that of human being-in-depth.

Men and women as creators of science and technology, culture and civilization, are today also the only possible destroyers of civilization.

Everything about human nature is a mystery. As Lincoln Barnett writes in his study of Einstein's contribution to modern scientific thought:

> In the evolution of scientific thought, one fact has become impressively clear; there is no mystery of the physical world which does not point to a mystery beyond itself. All highroads of the intellect, all byways of theory and conjecture, lead ultimately to an abyss that human ingenuity can never span. For man is enchained by the very condition of his being, his finiteness and involvement in nature. The further he extends his horizons, the more vividly he recognizes the fact that as the physicist Niels Bohr puts it, "We are both spectators and actors in the great drama of existence." *Man is thus his own greatest mystery.* He does not understand the vast veiled universe into which he has been cast for the reason that he does not understand himself. He comprehends but little of his organic processes and even less of his unique capacity to perceive the world around him, to reason and to dream. Least of all does he understand his noblest and most mysterious faculty: the ability to transcend himself and perceive himself in the act of perception.[18] (italics added)

This thought was similarly expressed by the mathematician-mystic Blaise Pascal in his *Pensees* [348]: "In space, the universe engulfs me and reduces me to a pinpoint. But through thought, I understand that universe."

Pleading for the viewing of humanity in its depths on the part of modern science, the eminent paleontologist Teilhard de Chardin says:

> When studied narrowly in himself . . . man is a tiny, even a shrinking creature. His over-pronounced individuality conceals from our eyes the whole to which he belongs . . . our minds incline to break nature up into pieces and to forget both its deep inter-relations and its measureless horizons. We incline to all that is bad in anthropocentrism. And it is this that leads scientists to refuse to consider man as an object of scientific scrutiny except through his body.
>
> The time has come to realise that an interpretation of the universe—even a positivist one—remains unsatisfying unless it covers the interior as well as the exterior of things; mind as well as matter. The true physics is that which will, one day, achieve the inclusion of man in his wholeness in a coherent picture of the world.[19]

The *Upanishads* of India discerned the finite aspect as but the outer crust or layer of the infinite and immortal person within. In our finiteness, we interact with the finite world of myriad changes around us. In this, one is a *speck of dust* in the vast immensity of space in which "the universe engulfs me and reduces me to a pinpoint," in the profound words of Pascal quoted above. But in our infinite dimension as the imperishable 'Self,' we can understand the universe and also transcend it. The dimensions of this, our inner aspect and, through us, of our environing universe, are slowly dawning on modern scientific thought.

Asking the significant question: "Up to now has science ever troubled to look at the world other than from without?"[20] de Chardin proceeds to explain:

> In the eyes of the physicist, nothing exists legitimately . . . except the without of things. The same intellectual attitude is still permissible in the bacteriologists, whose cultures (apart from substantial difficulties) are treated as laboratory reagents. But it is still more difficult in the realm of plants. It tends to become a gamble in the case of a biologist studying the behavior of insects or coelenterates. It seems entirely futile with regard to the vertebrates. Finally, it breaks down completely with man, in whom the existence of a within can no longer be evaded, because it is the object of a direct intuition and the substance of all knowledge.[21]

Most people, Indians included, did not know that India, ages ago, developed the higher part of what Julian Huxley has termed a "science of human possibilities." In the *Upanishads* and *Bhagavad Gita*, India fostered, and continues to do so to the present, the science of human being-in-depth or *adhyatma-vidya*. In the systems of Vedanta and Yoga, India cultivated the science and technique of a comprehensive spirituality encompassing action as well as contemplation. Indian philosophy sees no conflict between physical science and this science of spirituality, between the "known" physical aspect and the "unknown" inner spiritual person.

Apropos de Chardin came to the same conclusion:

> It is impossible to deny that, deep within ourselves, an "interior" appears at the heart of beings, as it were seen through a rent. This is enough to ensure that, in one degree or another, this "interior" should obtrude itself as existing everywhere in nature from all time. Since the stuff of the universe has an inner aspect at one point of itself, there is necessarily a *double aspect to its structure*, . . . in every region of space and time—in the same way, for instance, as it is granular: *coextensive with their Without, there is a Within to things.*[22]

It is high time that we today, particularly teachers and students, reorient our critical attention, interest and inquiry, and direct the searchlight of investigation into this fascinting and rewarding aspect of India's ancient spiritual tradition, into the mystery of this inner dimension of nature revealed in nature's unique product, namely, ourselves. If we do not acquire this strength of spirituality, we will have to depend more and more on external sources such as medical means for stabilizing ourselves. For clinical purposes such occasional external dependence is understandable. But to make it the normal pattern of human life is to drain life of all spiritual values. Although molecular biology is in itself a new science, it can be used for good or for not-so-good purposes. For humanity to surrender its human destiny to biological engineering techniques as the only way to stabilize human life brings it into great danger – that of converting human society into an animal farm.

That such dismal possibilities are before us due to a wholesale dependence on physical science and technology, is revealed in such books with grim titles as *The Biological Time Bomb*, by G. Ratray Taylor. The science that will do so will cease to be science and become nescience!

As we advance in our inquiry and research into the aspect of the human tradition referred to above, we will increasingly get a grip on the human situation through the reformulation and implementation of educational goals and processes. In this way, a happy synthesis of physical science with the science of spirituality will be achieved, resulting in total human enrichment, internal as well as external, qualitative as well as quantitative.

Says the renowned neurologist, Sir Charles Sherrington, in his book, *Man on His Nature*:

> Today, Nature looms larger than ever and includes more fully than ever ourselves. It is, if you will, a machine, but it is a partly mentalised machine and in virtue of including ourselves, it is a machine with human qualities of mind. It is a running stream of energy – mental and physical – and unlike man-made machines, it is actuated by emotions, fears, and hopes, dislikes, and loves.[23]

KINSHIP BETWEEN VEDANTA AND MODERN SCIENCE

Swami Vivekananda has shown that religion, as developed in India in her Vedanta, and modern science, are close to each other in spirit, temper, and objectives. Both are spiritual disciplines. Even in the cosmology of the physical universe, in the theory of the unity of cause and effect, in the unity and conservation of matter and energy, and in the concept of evolution, cosmic, and organic, the two reveal many points of contact. Unlike the super-naturalistic theologies of the West, the fundamental cosmological position of both Vedanta and modern science is what Swami Vivekananda calls "the postulate (of the ultimate reality) of a self-evolving cause."

Vedanta calls this ultimate reality "Brahman," which is a universal spiritual principle. The *Taittiriya Upanishad* [III. 1.] defines Brahman as a majestic utterance that will be welcomed by every scientific thinker:

> Wherefrom all these entities are born, by which, being born, they abide; into which, at the time of dissolution, they enter—seek to know That; That is Brahman.

To the modern scientist that self-evolving cause is a material reality, the background material or cosmic dust, as astrophysicist Fred Hoyle terms it. To the Vedanta, which views it also in the light of the consciousness revealed in its evolutionary product, namely, our human nature, it is a universal spiritual principle, the *chit akasha*.

In his very recent book, even the title of which is significant in this context, *The Intelligent Universe*, Fred Hoyle deplores the "strange aspect of science that, until now, it has kept consciousness firmly out of any discussions of the material world," and adds that "yet it is with our consciousnes that we think and make observations, and it seems surprising that there should be no interaction between the world of mind and matter."[24]

The emphasis is that, against nineteenth-century materialism, some scientists have now begun to acknowledge a spiritual dimension to human experience. This is welcome from the point of view of spiritual truth, which, however, stands on its own strength.

In her fascinating book: *Dialogues with Scientists and Sages: the Search for Unity*, Renée Weber raises this question and gives us answers from physicists like David Bohm and biologists like Rupert Sheldrake:

> Do we live in a meaningless universe where molecules blindly spin along through chance, as mechanics claim? Or is matter alive and—at least minimally—conscious, a participant in the "dance" of meaning, as both Bohm and Sheldrake suggest? The latter view may be the more appealing, but it is unproven.

Again, to Weber's question: "What is matter? What is a field? What is meaning?" [p. 105]
To which Bohm answers:

> It has been commonly accepted, especially in the West, that the mental and the physical are quite different but somehow related, but the theory of their relationship has never been satisfactorily developed. I suggest that they are not actually separated, that the mental and the physical are two aspects, like the form and content of something which is only separable in thought, not in reality. Meaning is the bridge between the two aspects. I'd like to mention DNA as an activity of meaning. DNA is said to consitute a code or language. It's read by the RNA. According to the content, the RNA reads various segments of the DNA and takes out the meaning, which is to construct various proteins. The whole language of geneticists is such that they're tacitly recognizing the role of information and meaning.

Weber:

> When we say "the RNA reads the DNA," is that the standard term?

Sheldrake:

> Yes, the DNA is transcribed into the RNA and the RNA is then translated into protein. [p. 109]

Further into the conversation, Renée Weber asks: "This dance of meaning in many dimensions is your idea of the meaning-field?"
Bohm:

> It's some kind of field, isn't it, because it is not located everywhere and it doesn't manifest itself locally.

Weber:

> It transcends the finite entities in it and explains them.

Bohm:

> Yes. To come back to the quantum field again, the information field, you could almost say the electrons are the difference between participation and interaction. If there's a common view of meaning, the electrons are participating in a common activity or common dance, whereas the mechanical view is that they are just interacting, pushing at each other . . . . [p. 116]

And again a bit further, Renée Weber probes with: "How does Rupert view this?" [p. 117]
Sheldrake:

> The field builds up the entities. What I am saying is similar to what David is saying. The field organizes the energy. The field and the energy can't really be separated. You can't have energy in a completely free-floating form. Both are important. The energy gives a kind of actuality or activity to something. The field gives it its organization. The two are related.[25]

Vedanta views that field of universal energy as the field of pure Consciousness. Referring to this spiritual kinship between modern science and Vedanta, Swami Vivekananda said at Chicago at the Parliament Religions in 1893:

> Manifestation, and not creation, is the word of science today, and the Hindu is only glad that what he has been cherishing in his bosom for ages is going to be taught in more forcible language, and with further light, from the latest conclusions of science.[26]

Although modern scientific thought does not yet have, like Vedanta, a recognized place for any spiritual reality or principle, several scientists of the twentieth century, including biologists like Teilhard de Chardin and Julian Huxley, as pointed out earlier, as well as David Bohm, Rupert Sheldrake, Fritjof Capra and others recently, have endeavored to soften the materialism of physical science and to find a place for spiritual experience in the scientific world picture. Even Thomas Huxley had termed materialism *an intruder*. In our century, this protest has come from great physicists also. Sir James Jeans found that the final picture of the universe emerging from twentieth-century physical science was one in which the notion of matter was completely eliminated, "mind reigning supreme and alone."[27] Astrophysicist Robert Andrews Millikan considered materialism "a philosophy of unintelligence."

Now that twentieth-century physics is turning to some degree its face away from thoroughgoing materialism, twentieth-century biology is not far behind it in this orientation. The whole of modern scientific thought is in the throes of a silent spiritual revolution. With the emergence of the challenge of mind and consciousness, there is need to develop what Sir James Jeans termed "a new background of science:

> The old philosophy ceased to work at the end of the nineteenth century, and the twentieth-century physicist is hammering out a new philosophy for himself. Its essence is that he no longer sees nature as something entirely distinct from himself. Sometimes it is what he himself creates or selects or abstracts; sometimes it is what he destroys. . . .
>
> Thus the history of physical science in the twentieth-century is one of a progressive emancipation from the purely human angle of vision.[28]

Teilhard de Chardin and Julian Huxley have found the spiritual character of the world-stuff successively revealed in the course of organic evolution. Biology, in its theory of evolution, they held, reveals what de Chardin calls a "within of nature," over and above and different from the "without of nature" revealed by physics and astronomy. Vedanta terms the "within" the "*pratyak rupa*" and the "without" the "*parak rupa,*" both being of one and the same nature.

When the significance of this "within" of things is recognized in modern science, the scientific "background material" will undergo a spiritual orientation and thus come closer to Brahman, the "background reality" of the Vedanta. The synthesis of the knowledge of the "within" and the "without" is philosophy; and it is what India achieved in her Vedanta ages ago as *samyak-jnana,* comprehensive or perfect knowledge of total Reality. Reality itself does not know any distinctions between a "within" and a "without." These distinctions are made by the human mind for the convenience of study and research and the exigencies of daily life.

Just as the different branches of the physical sciences are but different approaches to the study of one and the same reality, and just as all such branches of study ultimately tend to mingle and merge into a grand science of the physical universe, into a unified science of the without of nature, so the science of the "within" and the science of the "without" mingle and merge in a science of Brahman, the total Reality. This is how Vedanta views *Brahma-vidya*, the science of Brahman – the term Brahman standing for the totality of Reality, physical and nonphysical. The *Mundaka Upanishad* [I. 1,1] defines "*Brahmavidya* as the basis of every science." Says Sri Krishna in the *Bhagavad Gita* [XIII. 2]:

> The knowledge of the observed (*Kshetra*) – the not-self, and of the observer (*Kshetrajna*) – the knower of the not-self, is true knowledge, according to Me.

Dealing with the all-inclusiveness of this Vedantic thought as expounded by Swami Vivekananda, Romain Rolland has this to say in his *The Life of Vivekananda*:

> But it is a matter of indifference to the calm pride of him who deems himself the stronger whether science accepts free Religion, in Vivekananda's sense of the term, or not; for his Religion accepts Science. It is vast enough to find a place at its table for all loyal seekers after truth.[29]

In Swami Vivekananda's lecture on "The Absolute and Manifestation," delivered in London in 1896, we find this passage:

> Do you not see whither science is tending? The Hindu nation proceeded through the study of the mind, through metaphysics and logic. The European nations start from external nature, and now they, too, are coming to the same results. We find that, searching through the mind, we at last come to that Oneness, that universal One, the internal Soul of everything, the essence and reality of everything. Through material science, we come to the same Oneness.[30]

The *Srimad Bhagavatam* refers to this complementary character of physical science and the science of religion, with respect to human knowledge and fulfillment, in a profound utterance of Sri Krishna:

> Generally, in the world, those who are efficient in the investigation of the truth of the external world or nature, uplift themselves by themselves from all sources of evil.
> For a human being, particularly, one's *guru* (teacher) is one's own self; because one achieves one's welfare through (inquiring into) direct sense

> experience and (inductive-deductive) inference based on the same. In this very human personality, also, wise ones, who have mastered the science and art of spirituality, clearly realize Me, (God, as the one universal Self of all) as the infinite reservoir of all energies.[31]

VEDANTIC VISION OF EVOLUTION

In the beginning, before evolution, what was this universe? This question can be found even in the *Vedas* and later in the *Upanishads*. According to Indian thought, in the beginning everything was pure existence and pure consciousness, existing without vibration, *anid avatam*, as described in the famous Hymn of Creation, the *Nasadiya Suktam*. Western students of Indian philosophy have been inspired by this famous hymn of the *Rig Veda* [X. 129.1], a bold speculation about the origin of life. The last line of the hymn is: "Who knows whence came this creation? Perhaps the gods above may know, but even they may not know, because they were posterior to creation – how could they know?" This great hymn describes what the universe might have been like before evolution: *tama asit, tamasa guhvamagre* – "Darkness covering darkness existed at the beginning."

The whole universe was in that concentrated form which, in later literature, is depicted as a point, or a *bindu*. Those who have studied the *chakras* of the Tantric tradition will find representations of a triangle, another triangle, then a circle, and so forth, and in the center is just a dot, a point. That *chakra* is a symbolic expression of the nature of evolution. The whole universe was in a single infinitesimal point, one single *bindu*. Out of that it exploded. The first explosion, which is still continuing, making for the expansion of the universe, is in the Big Bang theory.

Those sages used two words, which are very significant in science and in twentieth century cosmology: *sankocha, vakasa* – contraction, expansion. The expansion goes on for millions of years, then a counterprocess sets in, and there is contraction. The whole universe goes back to that point. The difference between the modern concept of cosmology and the ancient Indian one is in the nature of the primordial material. In modern cosmology it is a physical background "stuff." Vedanta says that background "stuff" was pure consciousness. Out of that this universe expanded and evolved, materialized into a physical manifestation, transforming itself in various layers of the subtle, less subtle, and finally into the concrete molecular world in which we live.

The word for nature in Sanskrit is *prakriti* with its two aspects, undifferentiated and evolving into the differentiated. Vedanta views the entire evolutionary process as progressive evolution of structure and form, and ever greater manifestation of the infinite Self within. It is evolution of matter and manifestation of spirit. Twentieth-century biology has recognized in the first appearance of living organisms the emergence in a rudimentary form of the unique datam of *experience,* through the unique datum of awareness. The living cell, described by biology as *self-duplicating matter,* discloses the emergence of experience as a new value, which the immense cosmos never revealed in its billions of years of history.

This spiritual value of awareness "grows" as it were in richness and variety as we move up the evolutionary ladder, defining and enlarging progressively the datum of experience with its two poles of the experiencer and the experienced. The evolution of the nervous system discloses progressive development of awareness in depth and range, and consequent increase in the grip of the organism on its environment.

This awareness achieves a new and significant breakthrough with the appearance of humanity on the evolutionary scene. "Man is unique in more ways than one," said Julian Huxley. The field of awareness of all other organisms is, largely, the external environment and, to a small extent, also the interior of their bodies – the "without" of nature. Humanity alone has awareness of the Self, as the subject of experience, along with awareness of the not-self, as the object of experience, of both the "within" and the "without" of nature.

That is our uniqueness, according to twentieth-century biology and ancient Vedanta. Self-awareness, which neurology considers as the source of human dominance over all of nature, and which nature achieved through the evolution of the human cerebral system, is a new dimension of awareness with tremendous implications, says Indian philosophy, for our further evolutionary destiny as much as for the philosophy of our humanity and nature.

The Vedantic view of evolution and of humanity's uniqueness has been stated rather briefly in the *Srimad Bhagavatam* [XI. 9. 28]:

> The divine One, having projected (evolved), withhis own inherent power, various forms such as trees, reptiles, cattle, birds, insects and fish, was not satisfied at heart with forms such as these; He then projected the human form endowed with the capacity to realize Brahman (the universal divine Self of all), and became extremely pleased.

Evolution has revealed that the mystery of the universe stirs in us as the mystery of the Self. The mystery of the universe will ever remain a mystery until this mystery of the Self has been solved. Till then, all our conclusions about the real nature of the universe submitted by science, philosophy, theology, or logic will be speculative ventures yielding mere postulates and conjectures.

The Indian mind was not content to remain at the stage of mere speculation or conjecture in so important a field as the knowledge of the ultimate truth about humanity and nature. Her thinkers boldly penetrated into the world within, taking the facts of awareness and the ego as their cue, or, in the words of the *Brhadaranyaka Upanishad* [I. 4. 7], as footprints. And when they penetrated to the depth, they discovered an infinite and eternal reality behind the finite and the time-bound. They designated that reality as of the nature of (infinite) experience, and as of the nature of Pure Consciousness, of which the infinite varieties of objects and subjects in the world are but passing configurations. The *Brhadaranyaka* registers this approach and object of its search in another significant passage:

> The Brahman that is immediate and direct, the Atman that is the innermost Self of all.[32]

"That thou art" (*tat tvam asi*), proclaims the *Chandogya Upanishad* [VI. 8. 7], aligning the modern individual with the immortal divine. Again and again, the *Upanishads* reiterate this great truth. If a scientist has such a profound dimension that he or she can comprehend the vast universe in a formula given by thought, what must be the dimension of a human being as the Atman, as Pure Consciousness, as the unchangeable infinite Self? Reality that "remains undivided in the divided things and processes of the world," as the *Bhagavad Gita* [XIII. 16], puts it.

The mystery of the universe was finally resolved through the solution of the mystery disclosed within our own nature. The sages of the *Upanishads* discovered the center of the universe in the center of our being. Through that discovery humanity was revealed in its infinite dimension, and the universe was also revealed in all its spiritual glory. Realization of this truth is the only way to life-fulfillment, say the *Upanishads*. The *Shvetashvatara Upanishad* [II. 14] confirms it:

> When the self-controlled spiritual aspirant realizes in this very body, the truth of Brahman (the infinite Self of all) through the truth of the Atman, (the Self), self-luminous as light, then, knowing the Divinity which is unborn, eternal, and untouched by the modifications of nature, he is freed from all evil.

This and similar verses from the *Upanishads* communicate a profound joyous discovery, as can be seen from the language in which it is couched in that immortal literature. In reaching the ultimate in the Atman, they had reached also the ultimate of being and knowledge, peace and joy, the unifying Field of Infinite Experience Itself. Hence they communicated their discovery of the inexhaustible mine of *satyam*, truth, *jnanam*, knowledge, and *ananda*, bliss. In the struggle to realize this truth and the life-fulfillment it involves, they saw the true meaning of the entire course of cosmic and organic evolution, especially of human evolution.

The organism seeks fulfillment. That is the end and aim of all its activities and processes as maintained by modern biology. In the *Upanishads*, we have the beautiful concepts of freedom and fullness. We want to become integral and experience the delight of freedom, to enlarge the bounds of our awareness, to get *bodhi*, complete enlightenment as the Buddha expressed it, the great aim of human evolution. Education, science, culture, sociopolitical processes and religion are meant to increase and enlarge the bounds of human awareness and the range and depth of human fulfillment by increasing our knowledge of, and control over, not only the outside world, but also the deep recesses within ourselves. Knowledge is power in the positive sciences. It is still more so in the science of religion, the science of our inner nature, where the power that is gained is not only greater in human terms of quantity, but also higher in terms of quality.

HOMEOSTASIS: ITS SIGNIFICANCE IN EVOLUTION

Nature has endowed us with the organic capacity to understand the world as well as ourselves. In this regard, from the stage of the higher mammals up to our human nature, according to biology, nature has been developing and perfecting the mechanisms of a built-in equilibrium, themostatic to begin with and homeostatic later, within the organism itself. Dealing with the evolutionary significance of this mechanism, the English neurologist William Grey Walter says:

> The acquisition of internal temperature control, thermostasis, was a supreme event in neural, indeed, in all natural history. It made possible the survival of mammals on a cooling globe. That was its general importance in evolution. Its particular importance was that it completed, in one section of the brain, an automatic system of stabilization for the vital functions of the organism – a condition known as homeostasis. *With this arrangement, other parts of the brain are left free for functions not immediately related to the vital engine or the senses, for functions surpassing the wonders of homeostasis itself.* [italics added][33]

And quoting the significant words of physiologist Claude Bernard, that *a fixed interior milieu is the condition for the free life*, Grey Walter continues:

> . . . Those who had the privilege of sitting under Sir Joseph Barcroft at Cambridge owe much to him for his explanation of this dictum and its

application to physiological research. We might otherwise have been scoffers; for "the free life" is not a scientific expression. He translated the saying into simple questions and guided us to the answers. . . . "What has the organism gained?" he asked, "by the constancy of temperature, constancy of hydrogen-ion concentration, constancy of water, constancy of sugar, constancy of oxygen, constancy of calcium, and the rest?" With his gift of quantitative expression, it was all in the day's work for him to demonstrate the individual intricacies of the various exquisitely balanced feedback mechanisms. But I recall in his manner a kind of modest trepidation, as if he feared we might ridicule his flight of fancy, when he gave us this illustration of homeostasis and its peculiar virtue:

"How often have I watched the ripples on the surface of a still lake made by a passing boat, noted their regularity and admired the patterns formed when two such ripple-systems meet; but the lake must be perfectly calm. To look for high intellectual development in a milieu whose properties have not become stabilized, is to seek ripple-patterns on the surface of the stormy Atlantic."[34]

Homeostasis as a fixed interior milieu is not an end in itself. It is just a condition, a necessary condition, for life forging ahead to higher and higher evolutionary levels. The highest level to be reached is the perfect freedom of the human spirit, by detaching the new significant datum of the self from its organic limitations and making it realize its true nature.

Nature has achieved physical homeostasis for the human system. But according to Vedanta, one now has to achieve for oneself, by oneself, through the organic capacities which nature has endowed one with, a mental homeostasis, with a view to realizing the Atman that is behind the mind. After explaining that, through homoestasis, "the upper brain is freed from the menial tasks of the body, the regulating functions being delegated to the lower brain," Grey Walter significantly remarks, as previously noted, that for mammals homeostasis meant only survival, but for humanity, it points the way to spiritual freedom.

Relating this physical homeostasis of organic evolution to the mental and spiritual homeostasis of yoga, Grey Walter concludes:

> And once again, as new horizons open, we become aware of old landmarks. The experience of homeostasis, the perfect mechanical calm which it allows the brain, has been known for two or three thousand years under various appellations. It is the physiological aspect of all the perfectionist faiths—*nirvana*, the abstraction of the yogi, the peace that passeth understanding, the derided "happiness that lies within"; it is a state of grace in which disorder and disease are mechanical slips and errors.[35]

The struggle to go beyond organic pulls and limitations, to realize the freedom of the spirit in Self-realization, needs to be supported and sustained by a stable moral life. Only when this base is secured can one carry forward the struggle directly into the inner world, fashion relevant disciplines and forge newer instruments out of the psychological energy systems, among which a tough mind, *manas*, and a pure *buddhi*, enlightened reason and pure will, are the most important. This results in that second homeostasis already mentioned, which is acquired with the help of the higher brain after freeing it from thraldom to the organic system. In Vedanta and yoga, this second homeostasis is comprehensively called "*shama*" and "*dama*," discipline of the mind and discipline of the sense organs. This is beautifully brought out in the chariot imagery of the third chapter of the *Katha Upanishad*, where enlightened reason and pure will are presented as the charioteer of humanity's journey to freedom and fulfillment.

The state in which the mind succeeds in stilling the clamor of the sense organs, itself becoming pure, steady and still, is called "*yoga*." This is the inner condition that spiritual seekers throughout the ages have striven to attain, and which many have attained, and in which many have realized God, the innermost Self of all, as affirmed by Sri Krishna in the *Bhagavad Gita* [IV. 10]:

> Freed from attachment, fear, and anger, absorbed in Me (the one Self in all), and taking refuge in Me, very many people, purified by the *tapas* of *jnana*, or discipline of spiritual knowledge, have attained oneness with Me.

The same truth is likewise affirmed by Gaudapada in his *Mandukya Upanishad Karika* [II. 35]:

> This transcendental non-dual state, in which relative existence is overcome, has been attained by sages who were free from attachment, fear and anger, and who had gone beyond (the mandate of) the Vedas (i.e. of all scriptures, in view of their entering the field of experiment, and getting the experience of spirituality).

From the time of the *Upanishads*, about four thousand years ago, and probably even earlier, India had developed a full-fledged science and technique of this subject, *yoga*. In the words of Yama in his teaching to the boy Naciketas in the *Katha Upanishad*:

> When the five sense organs of perception remain steady, along with the "insipient mind," and even "discriminating reason" does not act—that is the supreme state, say (the sages). They (the sages) consider that (state) as *Yoga*.[36]

PSYCHOSOCIAL EVOLUTION

Our spiritual growth, human evolution as psychosocial, is a pregnant theme in modern society. It shows us how to rescue ourselves from the tyranny of the sensate and the quantitative, and from the prevailing stagnation of a crude materialism and worldliness, and helps anyone to continue the evolutionary march to qualitative richness and fulfillment, individually and collectively.

In a lecture on "The Evolutionary Vision," delivered in 1959 at the closing sessions of the Chicago University symposium on *Evolution after Darwin*, held to commemorate the centenary of the publication of Darwin's *Origin of the Species*, the noted biologist Sir Julian Huxley gave a spiritual orientation to the evolutionary process:

> . . . Man's evolution is not biological but psycho-social; it operates by the mechanism of cultural tradition, which involves the cumulative self-reproduction and self-variation of mental activities and their products. Accordingly, major steps in the human phase of evolution are achieved by breakthroughs to new dominant patterns of mental organisation of knowledge, ideas and beliefs – ideological instead of physiological or biological organisation.
>
> All dominant thought organisations are concerned with the ultimate, as well as with the immediate, problems of existence or, I should rather say, with the most ultimate problems that the thought of the time is capable of formulating or even envisaging. They are all concerned with giving some interpretation of man, of the world which he is to live in, and of his place and role in that world – in other words, some comprehensive picture of human destiny and significance.[37]

Further, Huxley revealed the trend of evolution at the human stage towards *quality*:

> It (the evolutionary vision) shows us mind enthroned above matter, quantity subordinate to quality.[38]

And in his essay on "Emergence of Darwinism," he summed up the goal of the evolutionary process at the human level as fulfillment:

> In the light of our present knowledge, man's most comprehensive aim is seen not as mere survival, not as numerical increase, not as increased complexity or organization or increased control over his environment, but as greater fulfillment – the fuller realization of more possibilities by the human species collectively and more of its component members individually.[39]

Then, pleading for the development of a science of human possibilities, Huxley continued:

> Once greater fulfillment is recognized as man's ultimate or dominant aim, we shall need a science of human possibilities to help guide the long course of psycho-social evolution that lies ahead.[40]

What is meant by "psycho-social" evolution? From the living cell up to Homo sapiens, biological evolution was motivated by organic satisfactions, numerical increase, and organic survival. But, with the appearance of humanity, these became, modern biology maintains, secondary. The primary motivation becomes fulfillment. Evolution itself becomes, at this stage, conscious and deliberate and goal-oriented, unlike the instinctive processes at the prehuman stages.

This revolutionary change is the result of the fully developed human cerebral system, by virtue of which the evolutionary process itself undergoes a revolutionary change: what was organic evolution becomes psycho-social evolution. Organic evolution loses its primary significance in the case of Homo sapiens, who is endowed by nature with the versatile cerebral organ, with the aid of which one can invent any instrument or organ needed more efficiently and quickly than nature could through its slow and wasteful evolutionary processes. Accordingly, in the view of biologists, evolution now has risen from its organic to the psychosocial level.

In a self-centered individual, as in all prehuman species, the psyche, or mind or soul is limited and confined to the physical organism. In a moral or ethical person it expands, goes beyond the limitations of the physical organism and influences other psyches of the social milieu and is influenced by them. This is the result of psychosocial evolution. What biology calls "psychosocial evolution" is what the science of religion calls "ethical awareness" and "social feeling," the by-product of the early phases of spiritual growth.

With the onset of this psychosocial evolution, people develop the capacity to communicate affections as a matter of conscious choice, thus revealing a higher dimension to the human individuality than what is revealed by the physical individuality with its organic appetites and choices. All ethical theories and value systems presuppose a distinction between a lower self and a higher self. The liberation of the higher self is what is achieved through psychosocial evolution or spiritual growth: it is renunciation of the lower self and manifestation of the higher self.

The initial focus of the human self is the ego, which now appears on the evolutionary scene and after the human infant is about two-and-a-half years old. It is significant to note that, till its appearance, the human infant is as helpless and dependent on the environment like all prehuman species and that, with its appearance, the infant begins to dominate the environment. A human child of four or five years of age can control and manage animals like horses or other cattle immensely larger than itself. Modern neurology attributes this unique phenomenon to the emergence of a new datum in the human child with new energies as a result. That datum is the self as the ego and the new capacities are imagination, reason, judgment, will, and so forth. Referring to this, neurologist Grey Walter says:

> Thus the mechanisms of the brain reveal a deep physiological division between man and ape. If the title of the soul be given to the higher functions in question, it must be admitted that the other animals have only a glimmer of light that so shines before men. The nearest creature to us, the chimpanzee, cannot retain an image long enough to reflect on it, however clever it may be in learning tricks or getting food that is placed beyond its natural reach. Unable to rehearse the possible consequences of different responses to a stimulus, without any faculty of planning, the apes and other animals cannot learn to control their feelings, the first step towards independence of environment and eventual control of it. The activity of the animal brain is not checked to allow time for the choice of one among several possible responses, but only for the one reflex or conditioned response to emerge. The monkey's brain is in thrall to its senses. *Sentio ergo sum* (I sense, therefore I exist) might be the first reflection of a slightly inebriated ape, as it is often the last of alcoholic man; so near and yet so far apart, even then, are they.
>
> The brain of lion, tiger, rhinoceros, and other powerful animals also lack the mechanism of imagination, or we should not be here to discuss the matter. They cannot envisage changes in their environment, so they have never sought to alter it in all their efforts to retain lordship of their habitat.[41]

Homo sapiens alone achieved this power of imagining or *imaging* ideas. And this power was not an isolated phenomenon, for within the increased area of the cortex of the ancestral organ, nature evolved capacities for a series of new processes: observation, memory, comparison, evaluation, selection, judgment, and deliberate action. And in achieving these, two things were achieved: First, discovery of the path leading to the processing of raw experience into knowledge, of knowledge into power, and of power into control and manipulation of the environment, constituting the not-self aspect of experience.

Second, a faint awareness of the reality of himself or herself as the subject, as the Self, behind the fleeting images in his or her mind, and the discovery of the road leading inward to the total comprehension of this new dimension of reality, resulting in the increasing liberation of moral, aesthetic, and spiritual values in life, action, and behavior.

This steady advance on these two fronts is the story of culture and civilization; it also typifies the march of evolution at the human stage. With the emergence on the evolutionary scene of the human mind against the background of self-awareness – and disciplined in the seeking and finding of knowledge of the Self and not-self in varying degrees – nature yields in increasing measure to one of its own products the control and manipulation of the evolutionary process.

In spite of the rudimentary self-knowledge, which gave a measure of control over the animal and natural world, the earliest Homo sapiens remained largely an animal in appetites and behavior. A little more of this self-knowledge, gained through reflection in the context of social experience, helped to increase Homo sapien's self-control and to become more fully human. This process, ever in operation in human cultures and civilizations and sociopolitical organizations, has led to present-day humanity with an almost total control over the not-self environment by means of an efficient technology, with a global sweep in sociocultural interests and contacts, and with a yearning for the universal and human.

Yet, the disparity between knowledge of one's own self and control over one's inner nature on the one hand, and the knowledge of and control over external nature on the other, in short, between moral efficiency and technical efficiency, confronts us with the most serious problem that evolution has so far posed. This is thwarting humanity's urges and efforts to achieve fulfillment. Neglected and unsolved, this problem may as well make humanity the only possible destroyer of its own civilization, of the fruits of evolution, and of the species to boot. In the meantime, individually and collectively, one is destined to move from one tension to another, from one sorrow and unfulfillment to another.

The only solution lies in the deepening and strengthening of the value systems, of moral and spiritual awareness. Biological evolution achieved a measure of this in the life of early Homo sapien's rudimentary self-knowledge. Social evolution, guided by human intelligence, advanced this still further. In other words, a physical and organic self, separated from all other selves, gave place to a social self, morally related to an increasing number of other human beings. The dynamism of human evolution demands that this education must continue till the individual rises from ego-centeredness to ego-transcendance, and from knowledge to wisdom. Referring to this urgent need to rise from knowledge to wisdom, Bertrand Russell says in his *The Impact of Science on Society*:

> We are in the middle of a race between human skill as to means and human folly as to ends. Given sufficient folly as to ends, every increase in the skill required to achieve them is to the bad. The human race has survived hitherto owing to ignorance and incompetence; but, given know-

> ledge and competence combined with folly, there can be no certainty of survival. Knowledge is power, but it is power for evil just as much as for good. It follows that, unless men increase in wisdom, as much as in knowledge, increase of knowledge will be increase in sorrow.[42]

As has been indicated, biology speaks of the principle of homeostasis, or homeorhesis, as clarified not only by Grey Walter but also by biologist Conrad Hal Waddington (1905–1975), by which nature effected an automatic stabilization of internal conditions in the organism of the higher mammals. This promoted the slow evolution of the brain until, in human beings, it perfected the higher brain. Humanity's higher brain was released "for functions surpassing the wonders of homeostasis,"[43] according to modern neurology, or to function as the most wonderful instrument for carrying evolution to its specifically human areas, such as psychosocial, or, according to Vedanta, the moral and spiritual realms.

The capacity and fitness of the higher brain to undertake and fulfill this high function is directly proportional to its freedom from the thralldom to the lower brain, from slavery to the sensory apparatus and its appetites and the pressures and pulls of the individual's lower nature. It is obvious that the higher brain, with its power of imagination and reason, may stultify itself by functioning as the tail end of the sensory apparatus and the lower brain. But it may also redeem itself, and become true to itself by becoming truly higher. It is ethical discipline, that helps the higher brain to thus redeem itself and become eventually the agent of the individual's redemption also. This is human reason and will in their true forms, what Vedanta calls "*buddhi*," the supreme instrument that lifts life from knowledge to wisdom and from bondage to freedom. Referring to the significance, through homeostasis, of this development of the higher brain, Grey Walter says: "For mammals all, homeostasis meant survival; but for man, emancipation."[44]

Thus, the spiritual growth of humanity is a fact. And the more we know of the science and technique of this growth, the better for us and society. Growth, both as concept and word, is of great significance and variable in its meaning.

We know and recognize two types of growth, physical and mental. These two types of growth are necessary, but not sufficient. There is moreover a third type of growth, most vital and significant, though least recognized. Without it the other two types of growth will prove a child's undoing, individually and as a member of society, and the craving and search for fulfillment will only result in unfulfillment and defeat. This is the individual's spiritual growth, or growth in the spiritual dimension, which finds expression in ethical awareness and social sensibility to begin with, and finds, according to Vedanta, its consummation in the experience of the infinite, universal, and divine dimension of one's individuality, the Atman.

The real Self of a human being, says India's *adhyatma-vidya*, the science of human being-in-depth as the Atman, is, as the *Bhagavad Gita* says, "inaccessible to the sense organs and sense-bound mind, but accessible to *buddhi*, or reason." That the ego is unreal, that one's individuality or selfhood does not consist in the ego, is the central truth also of Buddhism.

As David Bohm has said: "Ego-centeredness centers on the self-image which is an illusion and a delusion. Therefore it's nothing. In true individuality a true being unfolds from the whole in its particular way for that particular moment."[45] And later he says, quoting from Renée Weber's *Dialogues with Scientists and Sages*: "It is impossible to have true individuality except when grounded in the whole. Anything else is egocentrism."[46]

A human being achieves individuality by the strengthening of his or her ego; that strength of ego gives him or her the experience of the value of individual freedom. And this freedom brings with it energy and dynamism which, at that level of individuality, is limited to the service of the ego only. When the individual grows beyond using freedom for the service of the ego, only then individuality grows into personality. It is faith in ourselves, as we develop our personality with the deepening of our inner awareness, that brings self-esteem. This growth from individuality to personality constitutes the first stage of human spiritual growth, according to Sri Krishna's philosophy of yoga in the *Gita*; it similarly constitutes the early stage of psychosocial evolution, according to the philosophy of evolution, at the human stage, of twentieth-century biology.

This is to be found in *The Science of Life*, a voluminous digest of modern biological knowledge by H. G. Wells, G. P. Wells, and Julian Huxley, in the section dealing with the philosophical implications of biology:

> Alone, in the silence of the night, and on a score of thoughtful occasions, we have demanded: can this self, so vividly central to my universe, so greedily possessive of the world, ever cease to be? Without it, surely, there is no world at all! And yet, this conscious self dies nightly when we sleep, and we cannot trace the stages by which in its stages it crept to an awareness of its own existence.
>
> Personality may be only one of nature's methods, a convenient provisional delusion of considerable strategic value. . . .
>
> . . . The more intelligent and comprehensive man's picture of the universe has become, the more intolerable has become his concentration on the individual life with its inevitable final rejection. . . .

> . . . He escapes from his ego by this merger (identification with and participation in a great being), and acquires an impersonal immortality in the association, his identity dissolving into the greater identity. This is the essence of much religious mysticism, and it is remarkable how closely the biological analysis of individuality brings us to the mystics. . . .
>
> . . . The Western mystic and the Eastern sage find a strong effect of endorsement in modern science and the everyday teaching of practical morality; both teach that self must be subordinated, that self is a method and not an end.[47]

In London in 1896, Swami Vivekananda foreshadowed the thinking of the twentieth century on one's true nature when he said: "There is no individuality except in the Infinite. . . . We are not individuals yet. We are struggling toward individuality and that is the Infinite; that is the real nature of man,"[48] meaning both men and women.

The science and technique of spiritual growth, from the "convenient provisional delusion" of the ego to the true Self, is the special contribution of ethics, aesthetics, and religion. It provides spiritual nourishment to human beings when at work or at worship, when in society or whether alone. Work done in a spirit of service and dedication and reinforced by an inward penetration through worship and meditation forms the technique of spiritual growth, according to Sri Krishna's teaching in *Bhagavad Gita* [VIII. 7]:

> Therefore, at all times, meditate upon Me, and engage yourself in the battle (of life).

Introducing verse fifty-five of chapter eleven of the same *Bhagavad Gita*, Shankaracharya says [XI. 55]:

> Now is proclaimed the practical implications of the essence of the meaning of the entire science of the *Gita* designed to lead one to spiritual freedom.
>
> Perform work (in a spirit of dedication) to Me; make Me the supreme goal (of your life); be My devotee, free from attachment and enmity to all beings; such a seeker attains to Me alone, O Arjuna.[49]

The laboratory for this science of spiritual growth is life itself, with its twin arenas of work done without and meditation within. Temples, churches, mosques, or a room set aside for worship within the house, also provide another laboratory. More important than these is the laboratory of a trained and pure mind. Worship, rituals, and other religious practices form useful aids if they are not done as ends in themselves but as means to spiritual growth, as instruments of a dynamic spirituality, as a depth education for character.

DHARMA AS SOCIAL ETHICS

We cannot advance on the long road of our spiritual growth or psychosocial evolution without disciplining our urges for organic satisfactions. It is necessary to bring a certain measure of stabilization to our inner life through such discipline by means of our knowledge and efforts. This is the second homeostasis to be achieved over and above the first homeostasis achieved by nature for us. That is what is emphasized in the *Bhagavad Gita*, namely, "that yoga which is called equanimity" (*samatvam yoga ucyate*).

This discipline is indicated in the Indian concept of *dharma*, or ethical sense, which is inseparable from any ordered human society. Bereft of it, the individual becomes reduced to a beast, says Indian wisdom. *Dharma*, as the principle of integration between one individual and another in society, does not mean religion in the sense of creed, doctrine, or ritual, nor any scheme of otherworldly salvation. A mere accumulation of bricks does not constitute a building. It needs cement to unite brick to brick to produce an integrated structure. Similarly, a mere aggregation of individuals does not constitute a society.

There is an integrating principle that makes for the evolution of a dynamic and expansive personality out of a static individuality and that holds its members together. That principle is *dharma*. It stresses the idea of mutuality, interdependence. We need the context of other human beings for our very humanization. This is how Sri Krishna expounds *dharma* in the *Mahabharata: Dharma* indicates that which holds us together. It is an integrative force within society.

Indian spiritual tradition does not frown or look down upon pleasure or prosperity, but treats them as valid human pursuits. But it considers greed and delusion, arising from unchecked organic cravings, as unethical, because they are antisocial. And to restrain these two pursuits from becoming antisocial, it presents a third vital human pursuit, namely, *dharma*—ethical sense. It is this that helps all people, not just a few powerful and clever ones, to experience the first two, that is, pleasure and prosperity. The validity and creative role of pleasure is presented in the *Bhagavad Gita* by Sri Krishna, who is the human manifestation of the one divine Self in all, in his statement: "I am that sensual craving (*kama*) in all beings which is unopposed to ethics (*dharma*)." [VII 11]

Indian spiritual tradition refers to ethics, prosperity, and sensual desire (*dharma*, *artha*, and *kama*) as the inseparable group of three. It treats them as the universal warp and woof of all ordered human society, theistic, atheistic, or agnostic, and presents absolute freedom of the spirit (*moksha*) as the fourth valid pursuit. The pursuit of freedom of the spirit is an optional trans-social endeavor meant for those few who desire and who dare to go deeper into the spiritual dimensions of reality and realize their own true nature in all its glory. For all the rest, this *moksha* or freedom value is experienced as *dharma* or ethical sense within the limitations of the social context. *Dharma,* thus, is the confluence of the secular and the spiritual, of the social and the trans-social; and every sacred and secular literature of India sings its glory. Indian culture is rooted in and inspired by this great value. The mystical heights of Indian as well as of all other world religions are the expressions of this *moksha,* this trans-social freedom value and ideal.

It is an echo of this great value of *dharma* that we get in the concept of psychosocial evolution of twentieth-century biology and in its corollary concepts of *quality* and *fulfillment* as the criteria of evolution at the human stage. In the emphasis on detachment from the ego and the organic system and the cravings centered in it, modern psychosocial evolution echoes the ancient yoga of non-attachment (*anasakti-yoga*) of the *Bhagavad Gita.*

RELIGION: ETHNICAL VERSUS SPIRITUAL

A scientific study of religion reveals two dimensions of every religion, especially the highly developed world religions: religion as a sociopolitical expression and religion as a path to the experience of God, or any equivalent value, as in Buddhist and absolutist systems. The first consists of the do's and don't's of religion and the rules and regulations about food, dress, marriage, and other social customs besides myths, legends, and cosmological theories. These are the sociopolitical elements of a religion that find a place in census registers and demarcate one religion from another. These elements of religion do not constitute the science of religion, but are only historically conditioned sociopolitical expressions of religion.

All religions could be classified scientifically in terms of their content, such as *bhakti-yoga, jnana-yoga, raja-yoga* and *karma-yoga,* which constitute the second dimension of religion. Here we deal with the truly spiritual part of religion with its emphasis on personal morality, worship, and adoration, and the disciplines designed to ensure spiritual growth. These factors comprise the essential, invariable and the universal core of religion, while the factors listed under the first dimension above, form its variable and nonessential part which is, to be sure, also relevant, but only when it does not choke the spirit of what we call the "second dimension."

Indian tradition calls the second as the *"shruti,"* the truly spiritual and scientific dimension, and the first as the *"smriti,"* the ethnical sociopolitical dimension. The *shruti* is considered eternal and universal in validity, while the *smriti* is local, parochial, and temporary in application. Accordingly, the *shruti* represents *sanatana dharma*, the eternal religion or perennial philosophy, while the *smriti* represents *yuga dharma*, the religious expression for a particular age or epoch, which is subject to change. India, therefore, considers the *yuga dharma* constituent of a religion not only not applicable for all people universally, but, more than that, obsolete, irrelevant, and often harmful to its own people of a later age because of the changing conditions of life of those concerned.

Sri Ramakrishna expresses this Indian wisdom in a belief and meaningful utterance to the effect that the Moghul coins have no currency under the British East India Company's rule. Human and social distortions are the product of the dominance of these obsolete elements of a socio-religious tradition; they sustain the rigidities of social customs, antihuman practices, interreligious and intrareligious frictions, disharmonies, and persecutions, and the stagnation and stubbornness of human attitudes.

The fundamental message of all religions, however, derives from their central core of essential spiritual truths, which constitute their *shruti* element. These spiritual truths are impersonal, and therefore universal; they were discovered, not created, by the scientists in religion, the mystics.

The authenticity of these truths lies in their being experienced by spiritual experimenters, those who seek the truth, and *in their being capable of verification by others*. Explaining this authenticity with respect to the Vedas of the Hindu tradition, Swami Vivekananda said in the course of his address at the Chicago Parliament of Religions in 1893:

> By the Vedas no books are meant; they mean the accumulated treasury of spiritual laws discovered by different persons in different times. Just as the law of gravitation existed before its discovery, and would exist if all humanity forgot it, so is it with the laws that govern the spiritual world. The moral, ethical, and spiritual relations between soul and soul, and between individual spirits and the Father of all spirits, were there before their discovery, and would remain even if we forgot them.
>
> The discoverers of these laws are called *rishis* (sages), and we honour them as perfected beings. I am glad to tell this audience that some of the very greatest of them were women.[50]

The above description can be relevant only with respect to the eternal and universal constituent of Hinduism and of every other world religion. The only differences lies in that it is in the Hindu tradition alone that this distinction between the universality of the *shruti* and the limited relevance of the *smriti*, or of the traditional interpretations and applications, is fully recognized and applied, and that social innovators and religious prophets are not only not persecuted and killed, but are also honored and followed.

This blessing Hinduism owes to its important literature of the *Upanishads,* which is all *shruti* and with no touch of *smriti.* They are the only sacred books – both within Hinduism and outside of it – which address themselves exclusively to the discovery of spiritual truths, and lead people, irrespective of caste, creed, sex, and race, to realize them in life. Thus, they have created in India a dynamic and healthy climate of active toleration and harmony as the inalienable characteristic of Indian culture and life.

In the light of this *shruti-smriti* concept, we perceive a kinship of physical science only with that aspect of religion that is the spiritual path to God, the *shruti* constituent, and very little kinship with its sociopolitical expression, the *smriti* constituent.

The term *ethnic* religion emphasizes the dominance of the *smriti* element with its group exclusiveness and tribal loyalties. And it is this ethnic religion that stagnates in the course of time, resists social change, and collides with physical science and every creative social endeavor. In all religions, the ethnic element becomes in time increasingly centered in the priest and in the feudal power; that which is the universal spiritual element becomes centered in the prophet and the divine incarnation. Ethnic religion will persist, but, says the Hindu tradition, it must be subordinated to the spiritual, if it is to aid individuals in their spiritual growth.

KNOWLEDGE: TRANSCENDENTAL AND INTELLECTUAL

In the *Mundaka Upanishad* [I. 1, 3], we find this question put by an earnest student to a great teacher: "What is that reality, O blessed One, by knowing which we can know all that there is in this manifested universe?"

Is there such a unique reality by knowing that we can understand all the manifestations of nature, internal as well as external? Is there a unity behind this diversity, a One behind the many? To this question the teacher gave a very significant reply:

> There are two kinds of knowledge to be acquired by man; so say the knowers of Brahman. One is called transcendental knowledge (*para vidya*), the other is knowledge of an intellectual nature (*apara vidya*).[51]

Both must be cultivated. Of these, intellectual knowledge, says the teacher of the *Upanishads,* consists of the sacred Vedas, phonetics, the code of rituals, grammar, etymology, prosody, and astronomy. In fact it comprises what we today would call the "entire gamut of positivistic knowledge," including the secondhand knowledge of the experience of religion contained in the sacred books of all religions.

Here in this *Upanishad* we have a scientific mind of the highest order-impersonal and detached. There is no desire to put forth a cherished opinion. Truth alone is the motive power, even if that truth goes against one's attachments and aversions. The teacher says that even the *Vedas*, the sacred books of the Indian people, belong to the category of ordinary knowledge. Who would dare say that one's own sacred books are ordinary, except one who is of a detached and scientific frame of mind, who is in search of truth and not dogma; who has nothing to hide, no opinion to uphold, no prejudice to defend, who just wants to know the truth and is prepared to sacrifice everything else in the bargain.

No religion except that derived from the Upanishadic tradition has practiced this bold detachment. The follower of every other religion, if asked what is ordinary knowledge, would unhesitatingly reply: All the sacred books of all religions except my own. But this teacher of the *Upanishads* has the detachment and boldness, proceeding from the love of truth, to say that even the *Vedas*, held in such veneration by all, are secondary; all the sacred books and all the positive sciences and the arts are of a lower nature.

Sri Ramakrishna, in our time, re-emphasized this spirit when he said that the *Vedas* and all other sacred books, do not contain God, they give only hints, only information about God. They are like the Hindu almanac that contains the forecast of rainfall for the year.[52] But, added Sri Ramakrishna, by sqeezing the almanac you won't get a drop of water! Similarly, by squeezing the sacred Scriptures none can get God; but by squeezing one's own experiences, all can realize God; God being the one Self of all.

What, then, is left to be included in the category of transcendental knowledge? The teacher proceeds to indicate this elusive theme. There is a tremendous field of knowledge, an area of experience for humanity, still left, but it belongs to a different order. So the teacher pronounces the following: "That is the transcendental knowledge, by which the imperishable (Reality) is realized."[53] Physical sciences deal only with things that change and are perishable. As Sir Arthur Eddington has put it, science gives us "knowledge of structural form and not knowledge of content." The sacred books give us, in the words of Sri Ramakrishna, only *information about God*. And yet we feel with Eddington that 'all through the physical universe runs that unknown content." What is that content? And how can we get at it? If the positive sciences cannot get at it, there must be another discipline, another line of inquiry, which will be able to give us that truth.

If the sacred books contain only information about God, there must be a discipline that gives us God and not merely information about God. It is this inquiry that pervades the *Upanishads* and that has made them immortal even as literature. Let it be said that the nature and scope of that inquiry, the way it was conducted, and the truths gained from it, have something superb about them. There is no effort to uphold a mere opinion, however dear; no struggle to get a dogma across and cling to it or thrust it upon others. There is no trace of weariness or sluggishness of mind, seeking a resting place on the way. Truth, and nothing but truth, is the watchword. Suffused with the spirit of truth, the sages have declared: "Truth alone triumphs, not untruth; the path to the luminous Reality is spread out with truth only."[54]

The path to the luminous Reality is strewn with the debris of discarded opinions, pleasing dogmas, broken hypotheses, and even dethroned gods! Thought was not allowed to linger on any of these themes for long. It forged ahead on the two wings of *critical discrimination* and *inner detachment*, (*viveka*) and (*vairagya*), wafted by the current of a single-minded passion for truth. One sage puts forth a conclusion about the data of the internal world gathered by him. Another shows it as inadequate; this stimulates further inquiry, leading to a deeper pronouncement. There was an unwearied and joyous search by the most gifted minds of the age, engaged in a graceful conflict of minds.

The whole process reached its consummation in the profound discovery of the individual's imperishable Self, the Atman, and its spiritual unity with the Self of the universe, Brahman. The entire process was a happy voyage of discovery. Looking back, they saw that the steps left behind were also valid, and that humanity travels not from error to truth, but from truth to truth, from lower truth to higher truth.

It is in this context, against this background, that the Indian approach to religion becomes significant. From the times of the *Upanishads* to our own times, India has sought in religion not a finished dogma to believe in, but a method and a means to pierce the veil that hides the ever present truth behind humanity and nature. The *Upanishads* glowingly register this passion of the Indian mind to seek and find truth through a penetrating study of experience. In the appreciative words of the American Christian missionary, Robert Ernest Hume:

> The earnestness of the search for truth is one of the delightful and commendable features of the Upanishads.[55]

The sages of the *Upanishads*, after a critical and penetrating search into the depth of 'being' "by means of the subtle reason or (*buddhi*) that had been trained by the sages in the search and discovery of subtle truths," as one of the *Upanishads* puts it,[56] found that imperishable reality as the one and non-dual Self, the *Atman*.

The opening verse of the *Isha Upanishad* proclaims this sublime truth in a verse that has inspired the philosophy of the *Bhagavad Gita* and innumerable spiritual seekers thereafter: "All this universe, in all its changing forms, is enveloped by the Lord." The second verse of chapter five of the *Katha Upanishad* was introduced by Shankaracharya in his commentary in these words: "The *Atman*, or the Divine Self, is not a dweller in the 'city' of one body only; of what else? It is the dweller in all bodies." The verse itself reads thus:

> He is the swan dwelling in the heaven (in the form of the sun), the air filling the atmosphere, the fire dwelling on the altar, the holy guest in the house; (He is) in man, in gods, in the sacrifice, in the immensity of space; (He is) born in water (as the aquatic creatures) on the earth (as insects, reptiles and mammals); (He is) born as (the fruit of) sacrifice, born of the mountains (as rivers flowing from the mountains to the ocean); (He is) the True, the Infinite.[57]

This great verse, conveying a profound spiritual vision, occurs also in the *Rig-Veda* [IV. 40. 5], with the last word omitted. This is the vision that determined the Indian attitude to nature, whether physical, botanical, zoological, or the human environment. All of these and more were not regarded as enemies to be conquered or exploited as is now being done throughout the world, particularly by many in the West, but as friends to be understood, respected, and wisely used. Acting like an enemy, a person plunders and ravages nature. That attitude inevitably is transferred to human beings at-large, resulting in wars, colonial exploitation, and slave trade. It also produces serious ecological imbalances, until violated nature begins to violate and mutilate the perpetrator. This is the tragedy that is being experienced by modern civilization and is posing a serious challenge to human ingenuity today.

The Indian vision of the spiritual unity of all existence has, accordingly, been receiving responsive echoes from an increasing number of thinkers and scientists in the West during the past decade. Criticisms of the economics of affluence, of GNP as the false god of economic growth, of the unbridled pursuit of organic satisfactions, and the ravaging of nature, are increasing in volume and intensity. Books about nature, upholding the Indian point of view and quoting Upanishadic passages, are coming out in greater numbers in the West. One such book, published not too long ago, is *The Secret Life of Plants*, by Peter Tompkins and Christopher Bird. It is indeed a fascinating account of the researches on the subject conducted in the United States, Soviet Russia, and other countries. Concluding their introduction to the book, the authors say:

> Evidence now supports the vision of the poet and the philosopher that plants are living, breathing, communicating creatures, endowed with personality and the attributes of soul. It is only we, in our blindness, who have insisted on considering them automata.[58]

What is of special interest is its sixth chapter entitled "Plant Life Magnified 100 Million Times," containing a moving and vivid account of the pioneering work of Sir Jagadish Chandra Bose in this vital field, which was presented to the world in the first three decades of this century. In the opening paragraph, the authors present the Bose Institute in Calcutta as the "Indian Temple of Science" bearing the inscription: This temple is dedicated to the feet of God for bringing honour to India and happiness to the world.

Starting his scientific research (initially in the field of physics) in a small twenty foot square room for a laboratory in Calcutta and creating his own tools and instruments, Bose demonstrated the existence and propagation of wireless waves in 1895. His work in physics led him imperceptibly to botany and physiology, which convinced him of the tenuous nature of the boundary between "non-living" metals and "living" organisms and the "fundamental unity among the apparent diversity of nature." And on 10 May 1901, he addressed the Royal Institution in London, ending his lecture and experimental demonstration before a scientific audience, half-appreciative, half-skeptical, with these words:

> I have shown you this evening autographic records of the history of stress and strain in the living and non-living. How similar are the writings! So similar indeed that you cannot tell one apart from the other. Among such phenomena, how can we draw a line of demarcation and say, here the physical ends, and there the physiological begins? Such absolute barriers do not exist.
>
> It was when I came upon the mute witness of these self-made records, and perceived in them one phase of a pervading unity that bears within it all things . . . it was *then that I understood for the first time, a little of that message proclaimed by my ancestors on the banks of the Ganges thirty centuries ago*: "They who see but One, in all the changing manifoldness of this universe, unto them belongs Eternal Truth – unto none else, unto none else!"[59] (italics added)

The *London Times* responded to these experiments by Bose during his trips to Europe in 1919 and 1920 by saying that the East had swept the universe into a synthesis and beheld the *one* in its ever changing manifestations while England was still barbaric.[60]

The book ends with this paragraph:

> The attraction of the seer's supersensible world, or worlds within worlds, is too great to forego, and the stakes are too high, for they may include survival for the planet. Where the modern scientist is baffled by the secrets of the life of plants, the seer offers solutions which, however incredible, make more sense than the dusty mouthings of academicians; what is more, they give philosophic meaning to totality of life.[61]

The experiments and insights of J. C. Bose's research into the microscopic world is like a mighty beacon, a forerunner of today's research into the subatomic world. All the physical sciences are engaged in this search for truth, for unifying knowledge, through this capacity for insight. The very methods of science are based on this urge to unify human knowledge and experience. That insight enables physical science to take an inductive leap from the known to the unknown, to get new knowledge from old knowledge. This phenomenon has achieved new heights in quantum and relativity physics, where physical science has crossed the barrier of the *objective* physical realm of the observed sense objects or data, to enter into the strange new realm of supersensory realities and has landed physical science and modern humanity on the fascinating shores of the mystery of the observing *subject*, the infinite mystery of his or her own consciousness. This datum of the consciousness of the observer has now emerged as the profoundest mystery at the fartherest reach of modern physical science.

SCIENCE AND RELIGION COMPLEMENTARY: THE VEDANTIC PERSPECTIVE

Religion expounded as a verified and verifiable science has a message for all humanity. Physical science, employing technology, may build a first-class house and equip it with radio, television, and other gadgets. The social security measures of a modern welfare state may provide everything necessary for a happy and full life in this world. The owner may give the house such charming names as "Peace Retreat," or "Happy Home." Yet none of these can, by themselves, insure that the people will live in that house in peace or happiness. For that depends to a large extent on another source of strength and nourishment, another type of knowledge and discipline – the knowledge and discipline proceeding from the science and technique of religion. If we can muster the help of the positive sciences to create a healthy external environment, and the help of the science of spirituality to create a healthy internal environment, then there can be hope to achieve total life-fulfillment, not otherwise. This is the testament of the *Upanishads*.

But today this is not the picture that modern civilization presents. In this technological civilization, there is a feeling of being inwardly impoverished and empty in an environment of wealth, power, and pleasure. People are full of tension and sorrow, doubt and uncertainty, all the time. Juvenile delinquency, drunkenness, child abuse, suicide, and an increasing variety of other maladies and individual and social distortions, are ever on the increase. Why? Because we are not inwardly satisfied, but smitten with ennui and boredom arising from the limitations of our sense-bound Weltanschauung. Indian thinkers foresaw this predicament ages ago. Here is what the ancient *Shvetashvatara Upanishad* said about the modern age:

> Even though men may (through their technical skill) roll up space like a piece of leather, still there will be no end of sorrow for them without the realization of the luminous One within.[62]

Arthur Schopenhauer wrote more than a hundred and fifty years ago in his opus, *The World as Will and Idea*:

> All men who are secure from want and care, now that at last they have thrown off all other burdens, become a burden to themselves.[63]

Today, we are our own major burden and problem. We can tackle and solve this problem not just by going in for more positivistic science, more technology, more life's amenities, more sociopolitical or microbiological manipulations of human conditions, but by cultivating the science of religion. Says Swami Vivekananda:

> You must bear in mind that religion does not consist in talk, or doctrines, or books, but in realization; it is not learning, but *being*.[64]

It is in this sense that India understood religion, and it is this idea of religion that Swami Vivekananda expounded in the West and the East in his powerful voice. The end and aim of religion, as India's ancient teachers have expressed it, is the experience, (*anubhava*), of God, through the steady growth in spiritual awareness. That is the touchstone of religion. There is such a thing as the spiritual growth of the individual, step by step. We experience this growth, just as we see a plant growing, or a building rising step by step, brick by brick.

When we *live* the life of religion, not in the sense of narrow dogma, but stressing spiritual values and practicing spiritual disciplines, strength comes to us, consciousness becomes expanded, sympathies grow and widen, and we feel that we are growing into better men and women. It is only the strength that proceeds from such inward spiritual growth and development that will enable an individual to digest, assimilate, and discipline the energies released by the progress of scientific technology. Such a person alone has the strength and wisdom to convert the chaos of life into a pattern of peace and happiness and general welfare.

If the spiritual value system of religion is taken away from human society, what remains is simple barbarism. Ancient civilizations were destroyed by barbarians bred outside those civilizations. But modern civilization, if it is to go the same way, will be destroyed by barbarians bred within that civilization itself. What can save us from this predicament is a little "Christian love" in our hearts for our neighbors, in the words of Bertrand Russell,[65] or a little more altruism, in the words of the late professor Pitirim A. Sorokin, of Harvard University.[66] This love comes from the practice of religion as defined by the world's authentic spiritual teachers.

Swami Vivekananda gave a scientific definition of religion: "Religion is the manifestation of the divinity already in man."[67]

Now comes the question: Can religion really accomplish anything? asked the Swami; he proceeded to answer it in this way:

> It can. It brings to man eternal life. It has made man what he is and will make of this human animal a god. That is what religion can do. Take religion from human society and what will remain? Nothing but a forest of brutes. Sense-happiness is not the goal of humanity. Wisdom, (*jnana*), is the goal of all life. We find that man enjoys his intellect more than an animal enjoys its senses; and we see that man enjoys his spiritual nature even more than his rational nature. So the highest wisdom must be this spiritual knowledge. With this knowledge will come bliss.[68]

Is not our scientific and technological civilization of today ready for such a message? The need today is to view science in its proper perspective, the perspective of total human knowledge and welfare. This is one of several vital contributions of Swami Vivekananda to modern thought. Dealing with the complementary character of Eastern contributions to religion and Western contributions to science, he said in his New York lecture on Feb. 23, 1896 in the Concert Hall of Madison Square Garden on "My Master":

> Each of these types has its grandeur, each has its glory. The present adjustment will be the harmonising, the mingling, of these two ideals. To the oriental, the world of spirit is as real as to the occidental is the world of senses. In the spiritual, the oriental finds everything he wants or hopes for; in it, he finds all that makes life real to him. To the occidental, he is a dreamer; to the oriental the occidental is a dreamer playing with ephemeral toys, and he laughs to think that grown-up men and women should make so much of a handful of matter which they will have to leave sooner or later. Each calls the other a dreamer. But the oriental ideal is as necessary for the progress of the human race as is the occidental, and I think it is more necessary. Machines never made mankind happy and never will make. He who is trying to make us believe this will

> claim that happiness is in the machine; but it is always in the mind. That man alone who is the lord of his mind can become happy, and none else. And what, after all, is this power of machinery? Why should a man who can send a current of electricity through a wire be called a very great man and a very intelligent man? Does not nature do a million times more than that every moment? Why not then fall down and worship nature?[69]

Education has to enable all students to achieve at least a fraction of the synthesis of East and West, spirituality and science, contemplation and action. It is the science of spirituality, the supreme science, (*para-vidya*), that fosters in people ethical, aesthetic, and spiritual values, including the moral values associated with pure science. The harmony of all these values and the intrinsic harmony between science and religion, always upheld in Vedanta, became revealed in our time in the deep spiritual kinship between Swami Vivekananda, the representative of modern scientific and philosophic knowledge, in his discipleship with Sri Ramakrishna, the full embodiment of spiritual wisdom.

All such values emerge from out of the depths of the human spirit at a certain stage of human evolution and after the achievement of some measure of mastery of the environment by individuals for their physical needs. It is folly to believe or to expect that such values will automatically result from industry or from technological manipulations of physical nature or from the wealth resulting from such achievements. Protesting against this widely held folly, Bertrand Russell said in his *Impact of Science on Society:*

> The machine as an object of adoration is the modern form of Satan, and its worship is the modern diabolism. . . . Whatever else may be mechanical, values are not, and this is something which no political philosopher must forget.[70]

College and university education is called "higher education." But it is obvious that the spiritual education Swami Vivekananda received from Sri Ramakrishna should be considered the highest for it brought East and West into harmony, as well as the sacred and the secular, and religion and science, besides building strength of character and fostering infinite compassion. Education from school through university should lead to this highest level, if the objective of education is to be fulfillment.

Sri Ramakrishna's experience and example also make it clear that individuals can enter into and benefit from this spiritual education from any stage or level of their school or college education.

Wisdom can accompany, enliven and creatively stimulate knowledge at any level – primary, secondary, undergraduate, and postgraduate. It is also equally clear that, without a little of that wisdom, knowledge at any of these levels can in the long run become not a blessing but a curse to oneself and to society, a breeding ground of pride, selfishness, exploitation, and violence on the one hand, and alienation, loneliness, and psychic breakdown on the other. These ills have afflicted societies and civilizations in the past and led them to decay and death. Western civilization, too, is facing these challenges today. Inasmuch as India also is currently absorbing Western civilization at a fast pace and is already experiencing some of its bad side effects, the people of India will be wise if they, too, open themselves up to the eternal message of the science of human being-in-depth, (*adhyatma-vidya*), and generate a fresh capital of spiritual energy with a view to digesting, assimilating, and transforming the physical and mental resources of this highly technical age.

The modern age demands that we meet the challenges of life with the challenge of an adequate philosophy. Vedanta as a philosophy is not only unafraid of the advances of scientific knowledge, but actually welcomes it warmly. Truth is its passion. Like modern physical science, Vedanta promotes the critical inquiring spirit, along with detachment, precision, and the challenge of verification. No field of knowledge can foster these moral and intellectual virtues and graces unless it is on the track of impersonal truth and does not countenance mere personal or subjective fancies and satisfactions.

This scientific characteristic of Vedanta was boldly brought out by Shankaracharya while presenting the great theme of inquiry into Brahman, in his commentary on the *Brahma-Sutras* and while expounding the scientific frame of mind in his commentary on the *Bhagavad Gita*.[71]

In the *Brahma-Sutra* commentary, he makes a distinction between *vastu-tantra* knowledge, knowledge depending on and arising from the *vastu* or existing reality, and *purusha-tantra* knowledge, knowledge depending upon the *purusha* or person, that is, the moods, fancies and interests of a person.[72] Knowledge of an existing fact is independent of the knowing person; it is the discovery of facts, not knowledge creative of facts. On the contrary, knowledge depending on a person, is "susceptible of being held, altered or abolished, depending on the person concerned," as observed by Shankaracharya.

There is a vast field of personal human preferences, which constitute this latter type of knowledge, and they have their legitimate role to play in human life. But God and soul, as understood in Vedanta, are not mere subjective fancies. They belong to the field of dispassionate inquiry into and knowledge of "Brahman, immediate and direct, which is the innermost Self of all" as we learned earlier from the *Brhadaranyaka Upanishad*.

This truth of God or Brahman as the inner Self of all is the only rational sanction for ethics and morality. It is an ever present Reality as the knower behind all acts of perception and knowledge, who cannot be made an object of knowledge. Yet, to negate that knower is also an impossibility; for "He (or It) is the very Self of him who does the negation," as Shankaracharya says in his commentary on the *Brahma-Sutras.*[73]

This Brahman is not any extracosmic deity of the usual type met within a monotheism, which is only a logical postulate equally capable of being enthroned or dethroned by human reason, or maintained by faith alone but incapable of being verified. The Brahman of the *Upanishads*, on the other hand, being the one Self of all, is, quoting Shankaracharya again, "the very basis and consummation of experience, because the knowledge of Brahman is consummated in the experience (of Brahman), and refers, therefore, to an existing fact."[74] Brahman is unknown when one is in a state of spiritual ignorance, but is not unknowable, being the very Self of the knower and hence can be more intimately known than any sense object. This knowledge is obstructed and obscured by the self-not-self mix-up in normal experience, and calls for a discriminative inquiry.

The sages of the *Upanishads* realized through such a penetrating inquiry and search this infinite and immortal Atman, or Self, in themselves, behind the five ever changing sheaths: the body, the nervous system, the mind, the intellect, and the bliss of egolessness (as in deep sleep). In support we cite Yama, the teacher of Naciketas, the young student, we met before in the *Katha Upanishad:*

> This Atman, (being) hidden in all beings, is not manifest to all. But it *can be realized* by all who are trained to inquire into subtle truths, by means of their sharp, subtle, pure Reason.[75] [italics added]

We get an echo of this concept of the sheaths covering reality in the twentieth-century biology with respect to the first three. In the *Taittiriya Upanishad* we meet the phrase *tenaisa purnah*: "this is infilled by that." Compare with this "infilling" what American biologist George Gaylord Simpson is saying:

> A broad classification of the sciences into physical, biological, and social corresponds with three levels or organization of matter and energy, and not levels only, but also quite distinct kinds of organization. The three are sharply increasing orders of complexity, and each includes the lower grades. Vital organization is more intricate than physical organization and it is added to and does not replace physical organization, which is also fully involved in vital organization. Social organization retains and sums up the complexities of both these and adds its own still greater complexities.[76]

The impurities of the mind constitute the obstructions to the knowledge of this ever present divine dimension. These impurities are centered in the ego, in its attachments and aversions and bondage to the organic system. Search for truth, either in the external world, which yields scientific knowledge, or in the internal world, which yields spiritual experience, calls for the elimination of those impurities, which alone enables the mind to penetrate from the surface to the depths of nature, external as well as internal. It is the scientific spirit and temper that is highlighted in Sri Krishna's exhortation to Arjuna in the *Bhagavad Gita*, and which is amplified in Shankaracharya's commentary on the same:

> By the delusion of the pairs of opposites arising from attachment and aversion, O descendant of Bharata, all beings are fallen into deep delusion at birth, O scorcher of foes.
>
> But those with virtuous deeds whose impurities have been destroyed—they, freed from all the delusions of the pairs of opposites, worship Me with firm resolve.

Commenting on the first, Shankaracharya observes:

> For it is well known that knowledge *of things as they are*, even in the external world, cannot rise in the minds of those who are under the thraldom of attachment and aversion; if this is so, what wonder is there that knowledge of the inner Self, which is faced with many obstacles, does not arise in those who are enslaved by them and consequently are deeply deluded!
>
> Hence all beings, *whose reason is obstructed and deeply deluded* by the delusion of these pairs of opposites, do not know Me, who am their very Self, and, hence also, they do not worship Me as their own Self.[77] [italics added]

RATIONALISM AND THE MARCH OF REASON

Earlier we discussed the limitation of physical science as well as the limitation of dogma-bound religion, and referred to Swami Vivekananda's strong pleas to subject religion to rational scrutiny. In the wake of the materialistic world picture of nineteenth-century science, religion came under attack not only by physical science, but also by a philosophy and movement known as "rationalism," which had done good work to encourage clear thinking. But postwar rationalism has become somewhat anachronistic by continuing to swear by a physical science that is no longer what it was in the last century.

The humility of twentieth-century science is yet to invade the citadel of rationalism. That wholesome invasion will be accomplished when rationalism recognizes the distinction between religion on the one hand and superstition and obscurantism on the other. But today, its fight against all religion has, in the absence of this recognition, itself become an irrational venture. It can overcome this irrationality only when it grasps the limitations of the reason it handles, and recognizes the truth of the march of reason. It will then find that all the forces of religion are also on its side in the fight against every superstition and obscurantism.

What is the meaning of the statement that logical reason, which is the instrument of logic and scientific method, is limited in scope and feels baffled by the mystery of the external universe? That logical reason is inconclusive, (*tarka-apratishthatat*), is also a famous statement of the *Brahmasutras* of Badarayana. Reason is a precious value thrown up by evolution and the source of much human progress in culture and civilization. The discovery of its inadequacy is itself the result of our insatiable love of truth and of our passion to push forward in its search.

The discovery of the limitations of reason, therefore, is not, and should not be allowed to become, a signal to revert to unreason or less reason. It must be further developed into a more adequate instrument for pursuing the quest for truth. This is what Vedanta achieved in its philosophical reason (*buddhi*), as stated already. This is conveyed in a lucid utterance of Swami Vivekananda:

> On reason we must have to lay our foundation; we must follow reason as far as it leads; and when reason fails, reason itself will show us the way to the highest plane.[78]

Vedanta sees the chief basis of this limitation of scientific reason in its sole dependence on the observed sense-data of the external world and in neglecting the observer or experiencer of the inner world. Within the field of sense experience, scientific reason is the most versatile instrument of knowledge. We have, by slow degrees, developed this instrument along with its most important tool, language, in precision and range and have successfully dealt with the baffling and confused mass of data pouring in upon us from the external world.

With these great achievements to our credit, how can anyone speak with finality about the limitations of human reason? Have we not seen reason's limitations being overcome by reason itself in the brief course of human history? What a distance has reason traveled, from an uncertain tool in the hands of primitive man to an efficient instrument in the hands of twentieth-century scientists! Can we not expect, therefore, that reason itself will overcome whatever limitations have come into view in its scope and function?

The answer of Vedanta to these questionings is bold and clear and positive. Vedanta holds that reason is the most precious possession of humanity, that it should be kept bright and pure, and that nothing should be indulged in that weakens or destroys it.

What is behind the "march of reason" is revealed in the history of reason's confrontation with experience—with reason influencing experience, and experience, deeper and deeper ones, influencing reason. Reason as experienced in formal logic operates within the most rigid framework and has very little to do with experience. This fact explains its static and formal nature and its incapacity to come up with new knowledge. In all formal logical deductions, the conclusion is only a restatement of the proposition itself.

Reason gets involved in a direct confrontation with experience in the logic of scientific method. It was this discipline of experience that enabled scientific inductive reason, with the help of disciplined deduction, to achieve its great successes from the seventeenth to the nineteenth century in unraveling the mysteries of external nature. But, by the end of the nineteenth century, scientific reason began to feel even the framework of classical physics as too rigid for its expansive mood. Says physicist Werner Heisenberg:

> The nineteenth century developed an extremely rigid frame for natural science, which formed not only science, but also the general outlook of great masses of people. This frame was supported by the fundamental concepts of classical physics, space, time, matter, and causality; the concepts of reality applied to the things or events that we could perceive by our senses or that could be observed by means of the refined tools that technical science had provided. Matter was the primary reality. The progress of science was pictured as a crusade of conquest into the material world. Utility was the watchword of the time. . . . This frame was so narrow and rigid that it was difficult to find a place in it for many concepts of our language that had always belonged to its very substance, for instance, the concepts of mind, of the human soul, or of life.[79]

The breakdown of this rigid framework of classical physics, and of its reason, became inevitable at the end of the nineteenth century with the discovery of a mass of new facts regarding the physical world, more especially the subatomic world. The development of the relativity and quantum theories accelerated this process through the early decades of the present century, until the old framework became utterly untenable. The most revolutionary aspect of this change lay in repudiating the exclusively "objective" character of the so-called objective world studied by science, and the consequent change in its concept of reality. Pointing out the significance of the quantum theory in this connection, Heisenberg may be quoted as stating:

> It is in the quantam theory that the most fundamental changes with respect to the concept of reality have taken place, and in quantum theory in its final form the new ideas of atomic physics are concentrated and crystallized. . . . But the change in the concept of reality manifesting itself in quantum theory is not simply a continuation of the past; it seems to be a real break in the structure of modern science.[80]

The history of modern science reveals the distance traveled by reason from the sterility of formal logic, through the fruitful, though rigid, framework of classical physics, to the revolutionary and expansive heights of relativity and quantum physics. Every advance in the march of reason, every step forward in achieving reason's clarity and effectiveness, has been the product of increase in detachment, in subtlety, and in the range of facts.

The reason of formal logic rose beyond its own limitations by developing into the reason of classical physics with its stress on induction and verification. The reason of classical physics similarly transcended its own limitations by growing into the reason of twentieth-century physics.

In this latest development, reason achieved an evaluation of experience and a criticism of itself far surpassing anything that was ever achieved in the whole range of Western thought, scientific or philosophical. It is obvious that neither the reason of formal logic nor the reason of classical physics, which is the reason handled by rationalists and their rationalism, can handle the values that lie beyond the sensate level. For, that reason, as shown by modern depth psychology, is a fugitive in the hands of the unreason of the unconscious and the subconscious. Their limitations proceed from what Sir James Jeans calls their "purely human angle of vision."

Vedanta expresses the same idea by saying that their limitations proceed from their confining themselves to the data of the waking (*jagrat*) state only. In relativity and quantum physics – as also in other branches of science like twentieth-century biology and Freudian psychology – reason has broken through this rigid framework of the waking-state with its sense data and the ego, its synthetic a priori concepts, its limited ideas of subject and object, its notion of substantiality as the criterion of reality, copy, correspondence, coherence, and so forth, as criteria of truth. It has thus released reason from its sensate tether, or to use the Vedantic language, from its *waking-state* tether, through the study (again in Vedantic terminology) of the data of the waking and dream states in correlation.

The reality that confronts reason in the twentieth-century physics is not static objects in space and time, but dynamic events in a space-time continuum in which all objects and subjects of the waking-state become just passing *configurations* of that space-time. It is significant to note that it is this dimension of experience that is revealed in the dream state. If science finds that the subject or observer enters into our knowledge of the objective world, and if the purely objective is nowhere to be found—and this is the situation in nuclear physics—science would be true to itself, it would seem, if it initiated an inquiry into the unique datum of the subject, the observer, or the self, with a view to getting at the reality underlying all events and phenomena. With this widening of the field of investigation, the development and sharpening of reason has also to keep pace in order to cope with the ever subtler dimensions of reality. This could be achieved through greater and greater intellectual detachment and moral purity, arising from the liberation of reason, according to Vedanta, from thraldom to a human being's sensate nature.

When this is done, the logic of the conscious and the logic of the unconscious, the logic of the waking-state and the logic of the dream state, become fused into the grand logic of the totality of all precepts and concepts, (*drshyam*). The reason that comprehends this grand sweep of all concepts is the (*buddhi*), or philosophical reason, or wisdom, of the Vedanta, which alone has the capacity to turn its searchlight on the subject, seer, or the observer, behind all concepts. The answer to the question, what is the "known" cannot be found until the answer to the question of who is the "knower" is found. Scientific reason has already established the relative character of all objects experienced in the waking-state, as also of its ideas of time, space, and causality.

As configurations of the space-time continuum, space and time had been interpreted by relativity physics as possesing some reality which, in their separate forms, was denied them. The study of dreams similarly reveals the unreality of the separate dream presentations and the reality of the mind-stuff, (*chitta*). It is this investigation and its further pursuits, says Vedanta, that opens the way to developing scientific reason into philosophical reason.

Philosophical reason not only discovers the relativity, finitude, and changeability of all concepts, including the egos of the waking and dream states, but it also asks the fundamental philosophical question whether there is a changeless reality somewhere in the depth of experience, and if there is such a reality, what is its nature and what is its relation to the entire world of concepts and precepts. Knowledge and memory are data that demand the unity and unchangeability of the knowing subject or self; but the egos of the waking and dream states are changeable and mutually exclusive.

Does experience disclose a changeless subject beyond the egos of the two states? For seeking an answer to this vital question, Vedantic reason finds it necessary to investigate the philosophical significance of the third state apart from the two, waking and dream, namely, dreamless sleep, (*susupti*), in which all the subjects and objects of the other two states disappear and merge in the one eternal subject, which is of the nature of pure Consciousness, the Atman or Brahman, and of which the whole world of presentations with its subjects and objects are but passing configurations.

Vedanta insists that this insight into what dreamless sleep reveals comes to reason only when it becomes pure by shedding its last and persistent attachment, namely, the causal notion of the waking-state, a notion, which, even in the waking-state, is found to be untenable by quantum physics. The Reality that then shines is described by Vedanta as the *turiya*, the transcendental, which the *Mandukya Upanishad*, in its verse seven, describes as:

> Unseen, not caught in the network of relativity, ungrasped (by speech and all other sense organs), without any indicating marks (which alone makes logical inference possible), ungrasped by thought, without any name (for identification), of the essence of the consciousness of the unity of the Self, the tranquillisation of the ever-changing world phenomena, (all) peace, goodness, and non-duality—that is considered as the *turiya*, or the fourth—That is the Atman; That is to be realized.[81]

The Atman is thus the unity of all experience. This entire universe is the Atman, which is of the nature of *chit*, or pure Consciousness. Being the Self of all, Atman is *chit-svarupam*, of the very nature of pure Consciousness, and infinite and non-dual. Says the nuclear physicist Erwin Schroedinger on the nature of consciousness in *What is Life?*:

> Consciousness is never experienced in the plural, only in the singular. . . . Conciousness is a singular of which the plural is unknown; that there is only one thing and that, what seems to be a plurality, is merely a series of different aspects of this one thing, produced by a deception (the Indian *Maya*).[82]

It was this transcendent Consciousness, or *lokottara*, that the Buddha realized on that blessed full moon night over twenty-five hundred years ago. Referring to this realization, he told his disciples later:

> I attained the supreme peace of an ego-extinction not affected by decay. . . . disease, . . . death, . . . grief, . . . and defilement. And the *jnanam*, or knowledge, now as a thing perceived (*darshanam*), arose in me: My *vim-*

utti, or liberation, is established; *jati*, or subjection to the causal chain, is terminated here in this birth; there is now no re-birth.[83]

Furthermore:

> Hearken, monks, the *amrtam*, the Immortal, has been gained by me. I teach. I show the Truth.[84]

In the course of another discourse in the Jeta Grove of Sravasti, Buddha uttered these solemn words clarifying the *nirvana* experience of this transcendental state:

> There is, brethren, an unborn, a not-become, a not-made, a not-compounded. If there were not, brethren, this that is unborn, not become, not made, not compounded, there could not be made any escape from what is born, become, made, compounded.
>
> But since, brethren, there is this unborn, not-become, not-made, not-compounded, therefore is there made known an escape from what is born, become, made, compounded.[85]

In his *Mandukyo'panishad Karika*, Gaudapada refers to Brahman as pure Consciousness and as above causality:

> The knowledge (*Jnanam*) which is unborn and free from all imaginations is ever inseparable from the knowable. The immutable and birthless Brahman is the sole object of knowledge. The birthless is known by the birthless.[86]

And, making his obeisance to the human *guru*, who has realized the highest truth of the unity of all experience as the Self, which is beyond all cause and effect relations, Gaudapada says:

> I bow down to the best among men, who, with his knowledge, which as Pure Consciousness, is infinite like the Void, has realized the non-separateness of the objects and entities of the universe, which are also infinite like the Void, from the Knowable, i.e., Brahman.[87]

In the words of Sri Ramakrishna: "Pure Mind, Pure Intelligence, Pure Atman are one and the same thing (Reality)."[88] The *Brhadaranyaka Upanishad*, in a majestic passage, describes the *pranas*, or the energies of the world, as relative truth, and presents the *Atman* as the Absolute Truth:

> As the spider moves along the thread of the web produced by it from itself, and as from a blazing fire, tiny sparks fly in all directions, so from this *Atman* emanate all energies, all worlds, all luminous beings, and all entities. Its mystical name is—"Truth of truth." The cosmic energies (*prana*) are the relative truth; and *Atman* is the Absolute Truth of those energies.[89]

The scientific method that reason pursues in order to realize this ever present unity is described in the Vedanta as the methodology of the three states. This is reason comprehending all reality, external and internal, objective and subjective, the "without" and the "within" of all nature.

It is because of the very limited nature of the reason in rationalism that it is unable to distinguish between spirituality and superstition and, with overconfidence fights with both. And it is because reason in twentieth-century science has become expansive that it stands in awe before the great mystery of the unknown and is drawn towards it irresistibly.

Reason that sunders reality into scientific, artistic, and religious fields shows its own limitation, not that of reality. Such separation is permissible, as in the case of the different names of the same ocean surrounding the earth, in a provisional approach for purposes of study and analysis; but, if pursued too far and treated as final, it distorts reality. It is the supreme function of philosophical reason, says Vedanta, to synthesize the conclusions of the various branches of human knowledge and experience and achieve a vision of the total and integral reality. Reason in Vedanta achieved this comprehensive vision of reality and discovered thereby the ever present harmony, not only between religion and religion, but also between religion, art, and physical science.

The Vedantic vision of unity became, accordingly, the meeting ground of faith and reason, love and knowledge, poetry and philosophy, art, and science. Referring to this sweep of philosophical reason in Vedanta, as presented by Swami Vivekananda in the modern age, Sister Nivedita wrote:

> To him, there is no difference between service of man and worship of God, between manliness and faith, between true righteousness and spirituality. All his words, from one point of view, read as a commentary upon this central conviction: "Art, science, and religion," he said once, "are but three different ways of expressing a single truth. But in order to understand this, we must have the theory of *advaita*, non-duality."[90]

MODERN PHYSICS AND PHILOSOPHICAL REASON

In countless ways every department of physical science today is extending the boundaries of our knowledge of the fundamental unity behind the manifold diversities of the universe. Physical science started with the exploration of the mysteries of external nature, but at the farthest end of this search it finds itself face to face with the mystery of humanity and the individual, whose mind and consciousness are the deepest mystery of all. The philosophies of the East, particularly the Vedanta of India, including Buddhist thought, directly faced this mystery more than two thousand years ago, by initiating the exploration of the internal world and carrying it through to its depths. And today we are witness to a steady convergence of these two indirect and direct approaches in the gradual emergence of a common philosophy of the One behind the many.

Physicists of the first quarter of this century, faced with the challenge of the revolutionary discoveries of relativity and quantum physics, turned into bold philosophical thinkers, initiating the development of reason in physics into philosophical reason, by transforming it into a critique not only of the observed sense data of the physical world but also of the observer. Starting with Sir Arthur Eddington, Sir James Jeans, Max Plank, Albert Einstein, Erwin Schroedinger, Niels Bohr, Werner Heisenberg, and other great creators of the twentieth-century physics, the philosophical trend has grown in six decades, developing further in books like *The Tao of Physics*, by Fritjof Capra.*

Concluding his *Space, Time, and Gravitation*, Sir Arthur Eddington hinted at the emergence of the mystery of what we are within ourselves from the study of the mystery of physical nature:

> The theory of relativity has passed in review the whole subject matter of physics. It has unified the great laws which, by the precision of their formulation and the exactness of their application, have won the proud place in human knowledge which physical science holds today. And yet, in regard to the nature of things, this knowledge is only an empty shell—a form of symbols. *It is knowledge of structural form, and not knowledge of content*. All through the physical world runs that unknown content, *which must surely be the stuff of our consciousness*. Here is a hint of aspects deep within the world of physics, and yet unattainable by the methods of physics. And, moreover, we have found that, where science has progressed the farthest, the mind has but regained from nature that which the mind has put into nature. We have found a strange footprint on the shores of the unknown. We have devised profound theories, one after the other, to account for its origin. At last, we have succeeded in reconstructing the creature that made the footprint. And lo! it is our own.[91] [italics added]

Hints such as these, given by the earlier philosopher-scientists, have developed into positive affirmation as stated by Fritjof Capra. The very title of his book, *The Tao of Physics*, is significant in this connection, apart from the masterly and fascinating exposition he gives of his main thesis that "the basic elements of the Eastern world-view are also those of the world-view emerging from modern physics." Specifically he states:

---

*We are quoting Fritjob Capra at length because of his clear understanding of Eastern thought.

". . . Eastern thought and, more generally, mystical thought provide a consistent and relevant philosophical background to the theories of contemporary science."[92]

Noting that the image of science in the eyes of modern man has suffered much damage through two centuries of association with the philosophy of materialism and mechanism, and also because of contemporary reactions against the ravages of overtechnology, Capra seeks to restore the image of pure science as the discipline in the pursuit of truth and human excellence, not in opposition to, but in tune with, the spiritual heritage of humanity, more especially the spiritual heritage of the East:

> This book aims at improving the image of science by showing that there is an essential harmony between the spirit of Eastern wisdom and Western science. It attempts to suggest that modern physics goes far beyond technology, that the way – or Tao – of physics can be a path with a heart, a way to spiritual knowledge and self-realization.[93]

Echoing the voice of Vedanta and all mystical thought that the fundamental search for reality takes man beyond the senses and the sensory world of phenomena, Carpa says:

> On this journey to the world of the infinitely small, the most important step, from a philosophical point of view, was the first one; the step into the world of atoms. Probing inside the atom and investigating its structure, science transcended the limits of our sensory imagination. From this point on, it could no longer rely with absolute certainty on logic and commonsense. Atomic physics provided the scientists with the first glimpses of the essential nature of things. Like the mystics, physicists were now dealing with a non-sensory experience of reality and, like the mystics, they had to face the paradoxical aspects of this experience. From then on, therefore, the models and images of modern physics became akin to those of Eastern philosophy.[94]

Capra refers to the basic unity of the universe, as upheld in Eastern mysticism and modern physics, in these words:

> The most important characteristic of the Eastern world-view – one could almost say the essence of it – is the awareness of the unity and mutual interrelation of all things and events. The Eastern traditions constantly refer to this ultimate indivisible reality, which manifests itself in all things, and of which all things are parts. It is called *Brahman* in Hinduism, *Dharmakaya* in Buddhism, *Tao* in Taoism. . . .
>
> The basic oneness of the universe is not only the central characteristic of the mystical experience, but is also one of the most important revelations of modern physics. It becomes apparent at the atomic level,

and manifests itself more and more as one penetrates deeper into matter, down into the realm of sub-atomic particles. The unity of all things and events will be a recurring theme throughout our comparison of modern physics and Eastern philosophy.[95]

With both physics and Eastern philosophy speaking the same language regarding reality transcending space, time, and causality, Capra points out that there is a kinship between them:

> The space-time of relativistic physics is a similar timeless space of a higher dimension. All events in it are interconnected, but the connections are not causal. Particle interactions can be interpreted in terms of cause and effect only when the space-time diagrams are read in a definite direction, e.g. from the botton to the top. When they are taken as four dimensional patterns without any definite direction of time attached to them, there is no "before" and no "after, and thus no causation.
>
> Similarly, the Eastern mystics assert that, in transcending time, they also transcend the world of cause and effect. Like our ordinary notions of space and time, causation is an idea which is limited to a certain experience of the world and has to be abandoned when this experience is extended. In the words of Swami Vivekananda:
>
> Time, space, and causation are like the glass
> through which the Absolute is seen. In the
> Absolute there is neither time, space, nor causation.
>
> [Jnana Yoga, P. 169]
>
> The Eastern spiritual traditions show their followers various ways of going beyond the ordinary experience of time and freeing themselves from the chain of cause and effect—from the bondage of *karma*, as the Hindus and Buddhists say. It has therefore been said that Eastern mysticism is a liberation from time. The same may be said of relativistic physics.[96]

Later on he writes:

> . . . Subsequent to the emergence of the field concept, physicists have attempted to unify the various fields into a single fundamental field which would incorporate all physical phenomena. Einstein, in particular, spent the last years of his life searching for such a unified field. The *Brahman* of the Hindus, like the *Dharmakaya* of the Buddhists, and the *Tao* of the Taoists, can be seen, perhaps, as the ultimate unified field, from which spring not only the phenomena studied in physics, but all other phenomena as well.
>
> In the Eastern view, the reality underlying all phenomena is beyond all forms and defies all description and specification. It is, therefore, often

said to be formless, empty, or void. But this emptiness is not to be taken for mere nothingness. It is, on the contrary, the essence of all forms and the source of all life. Thus the *Upanishads say:*

'*Brahman* is life, *Brahman* is joy.
Brahman is the Void.
Joy, verily, that is the same as the Void.
The Void, verily, that is the same as joy.
[Chandogya Upanishad IV. 10.4][97]

Atomic physics is confronted with the problem of consciousness because of the datum of the "observer" or, to use the new and more meaningful term coined by the physicist John Wheeler, "participator." To return to Capra:

> In modern physics, the question of consciousness has arisen in connection with the observation of atomic phenomena. Quantum theory has made it clear that these phenomena can only be understood as links in a chain of processes, the end of which lies in the consciousness of the human observer. . . . The pragmatic formulation of quantum theory used by the scientists in their work does not refer to their consciousness explicitly, Eugene Wigner and other physicists have argued, however, that the explicit inclusion of human consciousness may be an essential aspect of future theories of matter.
>
> Such a development would open exciting possibilities for a direct interaction between physics and Eastern mysticism. The understanding of one's consciousness and its relation to the rest of the universe is the starting point of all mystical experiences. . . . If physicists really want to include the nature of human consciousness in their results of research, a study of Eastern ideas may well provide them with stimulating new viewpoints.[98]

Confirming the view expressed by Swami Vivekananda and quoted earlier, the physicist and the mystic reach the truth of unity but approach it from different angles, Capra says:

> In contrast to the mystic, the physicist begins his inquiry into the essential nature of things by studying the material world. Penetrating into ever deeper realms of matter, he has become aware of the essential unity of all things and events. More than that, he has also learnt that he himself and his consciousness are an integral part of this unity. Thus the mystic and the physicist arrive at the same conclusion: one starting from the inner realm, the other from the outer world. The harmony between their views confirms the ancient Indian wisdom that Brahman, the ultimate reality without, is identical to Atman, the reality within.[99]

There is thus no conflict between science and religion, between physical science and the science of spirituality. Both have the identical aim of discovering truth and helping man to grow physically, mentally, and achieve fulfillment. But each by itself is insufficient and helpless to give total fulfillment. They have been tried separately with unsatisfactory results. The older civilizations took guidance mostly from religion; their achievements were partial and limited. Modern civilization relies solely on science. Its achievements also have turned out to be partial and limited. The combination today of the spiritual energies of these two complementary disciplines in the life of humanity is eventually bound to produce fully integrated human beings, and thus contribute to evolving a truly human civilization.

The world is ripe and waiting. To this end Swami Vivekananda has made a most outstanding contribution. His synthetic vision finds lucid expression in a brief but comprehensive presentation of his Vedantic conviction:

> Each soul is potentially divine.
> The goal (of life) is to manifest this divinity within by controlling nature, external (through physical sciences, technology, and socio-political processes) and internal (through ethical, aesthetic, and religious processes).
>
> Do this either by work, or worship, or psychic control, or philosophy—by one, or more, or all of these—and be free.
>
> This is the whole of religion. Doctrines, or dogma, or rituals, or books, or temples, or forms, are but secondary details.[100]

This science and technique for realizing the true glory of humanity, which was followed with scientific thoroughness and detachment by the sages of the *Upanishads* and revalidated by a succession of spiritual experimenters down the ages from Buddha to Ramakrishna, is glowingly revealed in the immortal verses of the *Shvetashvatara Upanishad*, which can fittingly conclude this chapter on the similarities between science and religion: [II. 5, III. 8]

> Hear, ye children of immortality of the whole world, and even those that reside in the heavenly worlds. I have realized the Infinite Being (behind the finite world), luminous like the sun and beyond all darkness; by realizing That alone, shall one attain immortality; there is no other way to achieve the goal (of life).[101]

Faith and Reason in Our Scientific Age

Shraddha in religion is the basic reverential attitude that the unknown, the unseen, the imperishable exists behind the known, the seen, the perishable.

How many innumerable marvels has our technological civilization produced! For the future we can only speculate how the approaching space age will enlarge our one world. With the increase in technology, there is, however, an increase in problems of global dimension. Where there was once optimism, there is now despair. In face of this, are we in danger of becoming a cynical world-weary people, devoid of faith in anything and waiting for the world to end in a whimper as T. S. Eliot posited in one of his famous poems, "The Hollow Men"?[1] To have faith and to use reason in an age that presents unfathomable problems – that is the question. Our civilization is in need of both. For faith today in this scientific age has a vital bearing on the qualitative enrichment of human life and the destiny of humanity.

It may seem unbelievable that throughout the centuries India has never experienced the recurring conflict between faith and reason, which has been so characteristic a feature of Western history – as much in its history of science as in its history of religion. When we orient our minds in terms of the Indian tradition, we shall see not only these two, but also humanity's search for truth and life fulfillment in a new light, revealing the complementary role of science and religion in the great search.

In the whole cultural tradition of India, a watertight compartment was never made between reason and faith, sentiment, pragmatism, and so forth. The individual was taken as a whole. In the modern world, we have splintered human beings into various parts. We must bring the individual back together again. That is what is called today the "holistic tendency."

In various fields such as medicine as well as in education, the holistic approach is capturing the imagination. This is a good development at the end of this great twentieth century.

There is a beautiful word in Sanskrit for faith, it is *shraddha*. In the Indian tradition it is a hallowed word, a sacred word, and conveys much more than the English word – faith. In philosophical terms, the word usually used for reason in Sanskrit is *buddhi*. From the Indian point of view, faith and reason, *shraddha* and *buddhi* possess an intimate and inseparable relationship with each other in the search for truth.

There are those who have felt that these two are in eternal conflict with each other. Many have been taught in their schools and colleges that religion is based on faith and that science is based on reason. In the West this was, and for many still is true, that science is in conflict with religion and vice versa, and thus it usually follows that faith and reason are in conflict with each other.

This antagonism between faith and reason and the conflict between one faith and another has been prevalent in Western history from Greco-Roman times and even earlier. At the time of the birth and spread of Christianity in the Middle Eastern and Mediterranean regions of the world, there were many rival religious and philosophical factions. There were state maintained cults, state religions, mystery religions, Eleusinian mysteries, and other such, as well as Stoicism, Epicureanism, Platonists, Judaism, and Neo-Platonists—all with their points of view. The emphasis on faith was the message of Saint Paul. "The radiant life . . . " so Paul declared, "to be received through simple faith, a full trusting commitment . . ."[2] Other disciples of Jesus differed from Paul in their approach to the teachings of Jesus.

Faith, and its conflict with reason, became a source of great intellectual activity from the tenth to the fourteenth century. The problem of faith and reason was nothing new. Such Christians as Saint Anselm of Canterbury (1033?–1109), Peter Abelard (1113–1117) and Saint Thomas Aquinas (1225–1274) related faith and reason in varying degrees to each other. The ongoing point of view of the Catholic doctrine of faith had been: "As an act, not of insight and independent conviction, but of intellectual submission."[3] Beginning in the thirteenth century with Duns Scotus, a breach was made between faith and reason. Others followed and with William Ockham there was a complete separation. Earlier the theological ferment in Judaism, in Christianity and its culture had prompted the Biblical and Talmudic scholar, Moses Maimonides to write *The Guide for the Perplexed* for those confused by all the issues and puzzled by the conflict between religion, philosophy, and what might be called "scientific thought."

In spite of such thinkers as Duns Scotus and others, the development of religion in the West became a matter of a few dogmas and creeds that one was required to believe. At the time of Martin Luther, (1483–1546) increasing emphasis was given to dogma. One could not question these dogmas, but one had to have implicit faith.[4] Accordingly, reason's role was only to justify that faith. It then followed that science treated religion as outside the pale of reason, reason being the lifeblood of science. Faith continued to be a matter of intellectual submission. "The way to see by Faith is to shut the Eye of Reason,"[5] said the American diplomat and scientist, Benjamin Franklin in the mid-eighteenth century.

Such a dogmatic approach could not square with the spirit of science, which finds expression in an untrammeled search for facts, a critical inquiry into them, and in verification of the conclusions. Critical reason became the great strength of modern science. In Europe, primarily at the birth of scientific thought such as the Copernican theory, religion was powerfully entrenched in an established church. It had the authority to compel obedience and conformity. It tried to suppress this new spirit of rational critical inquiry, this spirit of emerging science. After some initial setbacks, science finally triumphed; reason rose to dominance and religion, based on mere faith, became defeated, after being initially treated as a dangerous error and finally discarded as a harmless superstition.

It was assumed in the last century, in the wake of the revolutionary advances of the physical sciences, that any knowledge outside the fields of the physical sciences could not be called scientific. It might be termed "private belief" or "faith," but could not be given the status of verified truth, which is science. The approach of the West to both science and religion gave rise to a whole host of dichotomies and irreconcilable contradictions such as natural *vs* supernatural, science *vs* religion, reason *vs* faith, and secular *vs* sacred. Western religion, on its part, carried these contradictions further into the field of inter-Christian and Christian-non-Christian relations as well.

It was unforunate that the organization of ignorance and prejudice against science came from established religion. But let not the truth be missed; this was only a Western experience. It was the product of the official Western approach to both science and religion. The approach of the great mystics of the West to religion, however, as of all mystics anywhere, was scientific in being experimental and experiential. But their approach and their voice was stifled by that dogmatic spirit and attitude upheld by the organized churches. The result was that the West could not, and did not develop a scientific attitude and tradition in the field of religion.

That explains its recurring experience of intolerance, hostility, and conflict, not only between religion and science, but also between Christian and non-Christian faiths, and between the various denominations of Christianity itself. Western approach to science in the last century, on the other hand, tended to equate science with physical science and to set up a permanent wall of separation between the world of facts and the world of values, denigrating the latter and impoverishing human life in a fundamental way in the process.

Even though twentieth-century science, in spite of its revolutionary advances, has found, officially speaking, no valid basis for religion, several eminent thinkers such as Theodosius Dobzhansky in biology, Gyorgy

Kepes in art, Abraham Maslow in psychology acknowledge the limitations of their fields to comprehend Reality and accept that there are various value theories.[6]

By the end of the nineteenth century, the West had become rational in the name of science, either skeptical or intolerant in the name of religion. At this critical junction of modern history, Indian culture produced great spiritual teachers like Sri Ramakrishna and Swami Vivekananda, who taught an inclusive approach to what religion is, to what humanity is, and the place of faith and reason. Today that approach is teaching us that this conflict between science and religion and between reason and faith is not a universal phenomenon and need not be.

India's historic experience over several thousand years reveals the powerful presence of a philosophy that sees truth and life in its integral wholeness and that does not allow such conflicts as had afflicted Western culture to arise and mar the beauty of human life and the goal of human fulfillment. The light of that philosophy is slowly helping people to realize that such conflicts are limited to particular cultural experiences and are not universal. That realization is to be achieved by all people today. We need to attain an insight into, and get a grip on, this inclusive approach to the problem of the relationship between faith and reason, between religion and science.

It was unfortunate that in Western culture, religion did not accept the spirit of critical inquiry. The West was then compelled to cultivate reason and physical science as an independent and exclusive pursuit. Such a development produced a mood which said we don't want religion, we don't want to have anything to do with faith, we shall do everything through science and reason. That is the temper of the modern spirit. As Carl Jung felt this, so he said:

> Modern man abhors faith and the religions based upon it. He holds them valid only so far as their knowledge-content seems to accord with his own experience of the psychic background. He wants to *know* — to experience for himself. . . . Our age wants to experience the psyche for itself. It wants original experience and not assumptions . . .[7]

THE MODERN WEST'S DESIRE TO RESOLVE THIS CONFLICT

Although this Western mood has unfortunately influenced millions of people in all parts of the world, due to the high prestige of the modern West, fortunately, in recent decades, the Western people are not happy over this conflict and are in search of a new approach and a new reconciliation. Increasing numbers of religious thinkers and institutions in the West today are seeking to find rational and scientific foundations to religion by putting more emphasis on experience and experiment and less on creed and dogma. There are, similarly, increasing numbers of scientists such as the late Harlow Shapley, Erich Fromm, Carl Jung, Viktor Frankl, Roberto Assagioli, and others in the West, who tell us today that humanity needs religion and faith. Moreover, they hold that these are more important for individuals compared to physical science. They also insist that it must be a religion that can stand rational scrutiny; otherwise it becomes mere superstition or cheap magic. It won't be true religion.

But such an approach to religion is not available to people in the West from their own historic experience. As we find in many publications, they are now in search of such an approach in the Indian and other Eastern traditions. There slowly is growing an appreciation in the West that the Indian experience has been quite different in this field from the Western experience.

The modern period of history is described as a scientific one. Science is dominated by the spirit of critical reason, questioning, investigation. It is very interesting to know how this new spirit appeared and developed in the modern West during the past four centuries. The history of modern science records a typical episode that illustrates well the impact of the wind of change that was blowing over Western Europe during the latter half of the fifteenth century.

A group of scholars of Oxford University was assembled in its library hall and engaged in solving what to the participants was a momentuous problem in zoology, namely, how many teeth a horse has. They followed the method of the centuries old tradition for solving such problems, namely, reference to ancient authorities. The scholars vied with each other in taking ancient books out of the library and consulting their authors. The author most consulted was Aristotle (384–322 B.C.) whose authority, already binding, but still more reinforced by the patronage of the Medieval church, was unquestioned and supreme. When the scholars were warmly engaged in the debate, quoting authorities to uphold one's position or refute that of one's opponent, one young scholar quietly left the hall and, in a few minutes, came back, to the horror of all those present, leading a live horse; and stationing it in the center of the hall, he calmly addressed his fellow-scholars: "Gentlemen, you want to know how many teeth a horse has? Here is a live horse. Please open its mouth and count its teeth, and thus acertain the truth for yourself." The rest of the scholars were thoroughly shocked by the foolhardy audacity of the young scholar and condemned him for believing, and asking them to believe, that a horse could have more or less teeth than what Aristotle and other authorities had provided for it in their books!

But that young scholar, who had been affected by the prevailing scientific wind, was like the stone, in the words of the Bible, that the builders rejected but became the coping stone of the new edifice.

This is the new magnificent edifice of modern science, whose bricks are facts and not opinions and whose blueprint was provided in the newly defined inductive method, what Sir Francis Bacon (1561–1626) termed the "*novum organon*." It summoned people to study the book of nature ever held out before it and, to this end, to discipline the mind in attitudes and methods, which will enable it to read that book effectively. This is the scientific spirit, method, and approach that has succeeded in wringing secrets after secrets from nature with amazing rapidity and profusion. It has converted this knowledge into power, creating, in the process, an entirely new culture and civilization of worldwide dimensions.

THE SCIENTIFIC SPIRIT AND THE *UPANISHADS*

It will be very inspiring and heartening for all to know that, from the beginning of Vedic times, through the *Upanishads*, Buddha, and Shankaracharya, India has encouraged this critical questioning approach to nature and to humanity, and has developed both the physical sciences and the science of religion based on it.

The physical sciences, art, philosophy, and religion of India reached the Western world during the medieval period through the Arabs. The Indian numerals, transmitted by the Arabs, became in the West the Arabic numerals. In the same way was the decimal system transmitted. A famous Arabic scholar, Qadi Sa'd, of the eleventh century, wrote: "The king of India was called the 'King of Wisdom,' because of the concern of the Indians for the sciences and their distinction in all branches of knowledge."[8] It is slowly being recognized that ancient India made great contributions to the sciences of surgery and medicine, mathematics, metallurgy, physical cosmology, grammar, linguistics, town planning, environmental hygiene, and in other fields.

This scientific spirit can be seen particularly in the *Astadhyayi* of Panini, who lived according to the latest research of some scholars about the fourteenth century B.C. (about the fifth century B.C. according to earlier scholars), and who hailed from the town of Salatura, situated near the meeting point of the Kabul River with the Indus River in the land of the Pathans, now in West Pakistan. As a result of a penetrating study of the spoken Sanskrit language of the people, the *laukika* or *bhasha*, and of the sacred Vedic Sanskrit, through a meticulous classification of the data collected, and through laws and rules deduced from his own and earlier investigation, Panini built up, in that famous book, the science of linguistics along with developing the philosophy and grammar of the Sanskrit language.

No other language in the world, either before or since, has received this scientific treatment, which Panini and his predecessors and two or three successors gave to Sanskrit, and that, too, at so early a period of human history. He gave to each vowel or consonant a precise sound value, which made Sanskrit a truly phonetic language, and classified all the sixteen vowels and thirty-five consonants. In the words of the erudite German Sanskrit scholar of the last century, Theodore Goldstucker:

> Panini's grammar is the centre of a vast and important branch of the ancient literature. No work has struck deeper roots than his in the soil of the scientific development of India. It is the standard of accuracy in speech – the grammatical basis of the *Vaidika* commentaries. It is appealed to by every scientific writer whenever he meets with a linguistic difficulty. Besides the inspired seers of the works, which are the root of Hindu belief, Panini is the only one among those authors of scientific works who may be looked upon as real personages, who is a *rishi* in the proper sense of the word – an author supposed to have had the foundation of his work revealed to him by a divinity.[9]

In his book *India as Known to Panini*, Dr. V. S. Agarwala writes:

> Panini undertook a profound investigation of the spoken and the living language of his day. He applied the inductive method in discovering and creating his own material for the purposes of evolving his grammatical system. As a trustworthy and competent witness of linguistic facts, he cast his net so wide that almost every kind of word in the language was brought in. . . .
>
> . . . On the whole, one may say that Panini's grammar is related to Sanskrit like the tap-root of a tree, the source of its sap and vitality regulating its growth. For Indo-European philology, Panini's work has proved of inestimable value. For Indian history and culture, the *Ashtadhyayi* is a mine of trustworthy information throwing light on numerous institutions, as the present study is directed to show.[10]

How unusual and extraordinary is this application of the scientific method to language. Sitting in their forest retreats or in centers of learning, these ancient linguists worked their ideas to perfection, to make Sanskrit, in the words of Joseph Campbell "the great spiritual language of the world," as he said on PBS television during "The Power of Myth" in October, 1988. What gifted and trained minds these ancient sages had, by which they developed not only the physical sciences, but also poetry, the fine arts, and philosophy and religion. Their minds hungered for truth and beauty and goodness — (*satyam, shivam, sundaram*) and possessed a passion to work for universal human welfare.

This universal outlook extended beyond the boundaries of the arts and sciences to the religious immigrants from the Christian, Jewish, and Zoroastrian traditions, who were given free land upon which to build their houses and places of worship. It was the land of India that had the first hospital for animals. This concern for human welfare extended even to the battlefields where there were strict regulations for the contesting forces as we see in *The Bhagavad Gita*.

These *rishis* or sages developed a philosophy in the *Upanishads* known as "Vedanta," which they described as *Brahma-vidya*, or science of Reality, or *Adhyatma-vidya*, the science of human being-in-depth, and which they defined as *sarva-vidya-pratistha*, the basis of every *vidya*, or science, in virtue of its vision of the changeless and non-dual pure Consciousness behind all the changeful and diverse phenomena of the world.

The philosopher Gaudapada of the seventh century *a.d.*, who was the *guru* of the *guru* of Shankaracharya, proclaimed the glory of this unifying wisdom, in a famous verse of his *Mandukya Karika*:

> I salute this philosophy that has taught the well-known yoga of nonseparateness, which conduces to the happiness and welfare of all beings, and which is free from all strife of disputation and contradiction. [IV.2]

There was a versatility about such a mind. It sought truth both in the outer world and in the inner world. It did not divide its search for truth, or truth itself, into rigid compartments and say that physical science should be pursued with the aid of critical reason and experiment, while religion should be approached simply through belief. In every branch of knowledge, whether secular or spiritual, where there is a forward thrust from the known to the unknown, there was an emphasis by these sages on critical inquiry. And in all such critical inquiries, there was a high place for faith as well as for reason. There is a unique quality about such a faith as a complementary value to critical reason. But such faith did not mean mere belief, just accepting uncritically what was heard or said.

This critical approach is the inheritance from the Upanishadic tradition that Buddha had when he gave his address to the Kalamas:

> This do I say to you, O Kalamas; but you may accept it, not because it is a report, not because it is a tradition, not because it is so said in the past, not because it is given from scripture, not for the sake of logical discussion, not for the sake of a particular method, not for the sake of disputation, not for the sake of forbearing with wrong views, not because it appears to be suitable, not because your preceptor is a recluse,

> but if you yourselves understand that this is so meritorious and blameless, and, when accepted, is for the benefit and happiness, then you may accept it.[11]

So from the time of the *Upanishads* over three thousand years ago, up to our own time, India had such spiritual teachers, who were essentially great scientific investigators in the field of religion before they were to teach. They did not present religion, therefore, as a finished creed or dogma to be accepted without questioning, but as a subject of research, experiment, and experience, by each person, by himself or herself, because it deals not with just knowing, but with being and becoming.

We can see this critical, inquiring spirit as a flood in the spiritual and philosophical quest of the *Upanishads,* though it is also not entirely absent in the pre-Upanishadic Vedic literature. The sages of the *Upanishads* dared to ask searching questions about nature, about humanity, and even about the tenets and gods of their inherited religion; they also dared to doubt when satisfactory answers were not forthcoming. They thereby evolved a great science of religion in the *Upanishads,* in such systematized treatises as the *Yoga Aphorisms of Patanjali,* and in such books as *The Crest Jewel of Discrimination* of Shankaracharya, and the *Astavakra Samhita,* not in conflict with, but complementary to, the science of physical nature and also a philosophy, unifying the physical sciences and the science of religion, the macrocosm and the microcosm.

Reality is one, they said, and it can be studied in its two fields of external nature and internal nature. The challenge to the human search for knowledge and truth comes not only from external physical nature, but also from something deep within. Both these worlds are to be investigated, and both faith and reason are to be used in such investigations. We need to have faith in ourselves, in other human beings, and in the ultimate meaningfulness of the universe. Search for truth, which is often a cooperative endeavor, has no meaning without this many-sided initial faith, this *shraddha*.

Thus, faith becomes the very basis of rational investigation. Without faith, there can be neither high science nor high religion. Great scientists like Einstein tell us today that science needs faith, along with reason, just as India's authentic spiritual teachers tell us that religion needs the strength of reason, along with faith. But this faith, this *shraddha,* is different from our usual idea of faith, which is mere static belief, accepting everything that is said by any authority without subjecting it to evidential tests. Shankaracharya defines true *shraddha* in a beautiful passage in his *Vivekachudamani*:

> Understanding as *true* the words of the guru and the scripture, is called by good people as *shraddha*, by which the *vastu*, or "the truth that already is there," is realized.[12]

It is faith with a view to investigating the truth of what is told; *satya-buddhyavadharanam* means "ascertaining through reason the truth (of what is taught)." Any fool can believe; but belief is to be subjected to the test of truth. That is real *shraddha*, the capacity to convert belief into truth and into conviction. Many modern scientists have said the same thing. Here is a luminous sentence from Thomas Huxley, collaborator of Darwin, quoted by J. Arthur Thomson in his *Introduction to Science*:

> The longer I live, the more obvious it is to me that the most sacred act of a man's life is to say and feel, "I believe such and such to be true." All the greatest rewards and all the heaviest penalties of existence cling about that act.[13]

Suppose someone says that he or she believes that such and such a person is dishonest; can we say that this is a true belief before investigating it and finding it to be true? Without investigating, it is just belief, often false belief, or prejudice. Anyone can say "I believe" in that way; but it requires a tremendous mental discipline to be able to say, "I believe such and such a thing *is true*." That is *shraddha* in physical science, and that is also *shraddha* in the science of religion. The Scriptures say something, and you say that you believe it. The *guru* says something, and you say that you believe it. But the main question is: Have you proceeded from that initial belief to the investigation of it, so that you know it for yourself to be true? That is *shraddha*.

In the science of religion, such investigation is done by life itself, and not by mere intellectual cogitation and futile discussion. In life, it is necessary to have a few beliefs of this type, "I believe such and such to be true," which carry creative energy with them, along with many of the other types of merely, "I believe," which are static and smug. The former signifies beliefs transformed into convictions; and that is *shraddha*. As the atomic scientist Robert Oppenheimer expressed it, when in 1945 he wrote in a letter: "In the Hindu scripture, in the *Bhagavad Gita*, it says, 'Man is a creature whose substance is faith. What his faith is, he is.'"[14]

FAITH AND REASON COMPLEMENTARY

Here you can see the scientific and rational and human aspects of *shraddha*; and all physical science, all religion, and all human life itself, needs this type of *shraddha*. What does *shraddha* mean in the physical sciences? It means a faith in the inner meaning of the universe. A scientist cannot investigate nature unless he or she has a prior feeling that nature is worth investigating, that there is some meaning behind all the confusing mass of data being examined. Max Planck, the father of modern quantum theory, has said:

> Anybody who has been seriously engaged in scientific work of any kind realizes that over the entrance to the gates of the temple of science are written the words: *Ye must have faith*. It is a quality which the scientist cannot dispense with.[15]

Without that prior faith, the researcher cannot get even the impulse to undertake the scientific inquiry. This stimulus given by *shraddha* is brought out by Shankaracharya in another definition of the word given by him, namely, *astikya buddhi* which, precisely translated, means "the positive-attitude-oriented reason."

Viewing faith from the point of view of scientific reason, Sir Arthur Eddington wrote: "In the age of reason, faith yet remains supreme; for reason is one of the articles of faith."[16]

In a frequently quoted passage, Albert Einstein says in his essay on "Science and Religion":

> Now, even though the realms of religion and science in themselves are clearly marked off from each other, nevertheless, there exist between the two strong reciprocal relationships and dependencies. Though religion may be that which determines the goal, it has, nevertheless, learned from science, in the broadest sense, what means will contribute to the attainment of the goals it has set up. But science can only be created by those who are thoroughly imbued with the aspiration towards truth and understanding. This source of feeling, however, springs from the sphere of religion. To this there also belongs the faith in the possibility that the regulations valid for the world of existence are rational, that is, comprehensible to reason. I cannot conceive of a genuine scientist without that profound faith. The situation may be expressed by an image: science without religion is lame, religion without science is blind.[17]

When the *Katha Upanishad* introduces its young boy, Nachiketas, inspired by a passion for truth and nothing but the truth, it presents him as "possessed" by *shraddha*. What does that *shraddha* mean? Does it mean that he believed in all the absurd stories told him by his elders? Not at all. He was in search of truth, and he had a deep faith that a profound truth lay behind the diverse phenomena of nature and life. Nachiketas' mind was thus exactly like the mind of a scientist face-to-face with the problem of the mystery of nature—the positive attitude of mind: (*astikya buddhi*), which is deeply convinced that there is truth hidden somewhere in the recesses of life: I am convinced of it, I am in search of it; I have not seen it yet, but I believe it is there. Otherwise, why should I dedicate my precious life to this arduous search, if I knew in advance that there was no truth hidden in life?

The known world I can see and experience with my senses: the unknown I do not see or know; and yet I feel it is there. This basic positive attitude toward the unknown dimension of reality is called *"shraddha."* No scientist can enter the field of scientific quest, much less discover any truth in that field, and no science can progress, without this positive attitude. So, in Vedanta, we emphasize the need for this *shraddha*, the need for a positive attitude toward the meaningfulness of the world around you and in you, for this faith in your capacity to unravel this mystery, and for a sincere and sustained search in that direction. This is absolutely essential.

The opposite of *shraddha* will make us understand better its true meaning and significance. In Sanskrit it is called *"a-shraddha,"* just the initial addition of *a*, to indicate the negative. In English, the attitude conveyed by this *ashraddha*, this no-faith, in its fullest form, is expressed by a powerful word, namely, cynicism. This cynical attitude is characteristic of one who has no faith in himself or herself, nor in the world. The mind is afflicted with a totality of negative attitudes, whereas *shraddha* signifies a totality of positive attitudes, which is what Shankaracharya conveys by the term *astikya buddhi*. This expresses the freshness and curiosity of a child's mind, while the other reflects the jaded and battered mind of defeated old age.

Cynicism spells the spiritual death of not only an individual, but of humanity. It scorns all values. It is the final nemesis of all civilizations rooted in a thoroughgoing materialism. It has afflicted, more or less, every civilization in the past, but it has become the prevailing attitude of modern Western civilization. It sets in when humanity is spiritually weakened through an overemphasis on material things and organic satisfactions, and through the consequent neglect of the ever present datum of the divine spark in people and nature. The individual, then, loses the spiritual capacity of digesting experiences. One is, by contrast, digested by one's experience in the world, and this results in cynicism. Many intellectuals the world over have developed this cynical attitude today. They have lost this precious value of *shraddha* and have become victims of its opposite, *ashraddha*.

At no time in history has there been such a pervasive cynical attitude as we find in this modern age. Almost every intellectual is partly or wholly a cynic. And, unlike in older civilizations in which cynicism afflicted only some people in old age, and that, too, due to too much rough handling by life, in modern civilization, it has started afflicting even children. Why? Because that basic *shraddha*, which is behind all true pursuits of knowledge and excellence, is missing. In addition, applied science has helped to sharpen modern humanity's craving for organic satisfactions beyond healthy levels. The intellect has become keen and clever—it can shake or upset or destroy beliefs, our own or that of others. But it has lost to an unbelievable degree the impulse to strive for truth, achieve goodness, or create and enjoy beauty. By seeming to know too much, and by draining away the faith in the meaningfulness of the deepest levels of life, it has dried up the springs of knowledge, abandoned all further search for truth, been entrapped at the organic level of life, and reduced itself to boredom and frustration. Is it any wonder that the drug culture is expanding everywhere? This cynicism is the surest index of the decay of a civilization, of its utter insufficiency, its spiritual poverty.

Somebody, perhaps it was Oscar Wilde, has defined a cynic in one sentence: "A cynic is one who knows the price of everything and the value of nothing."[18] Such a person knows all and everything, but does not have insight into the value of anything. A value system lies at a deeper level. To sense it, there is need for this positive attitude indicated by the word *shraddha*. A scientist may be a cynic in other fields of life, but in his or her own field of research he or she has a positive attitude. There is one scientist for whom this positive attitude, not only toward his field of research but also toward life, is especially true. Overcoming a severe handicap, Stephen Hawking, an astrophysicist, became interested, while doing research on general relativity, in black holes. He found that they could be expected to radiate gamma rays and X-rays. Interviewed by Bryant Gumbel on "Today Show" in New York City on NBC-TV on April 4, 1988, Stephen Hawking said: "To discover something new about the universe. That is a tremendous joy."

Cynical minds drain away all feeling and emotion and are just logical, assessing people and things with cold logic. This type of cold, logical, utilitarian attitude is infecting millions of people today, due to the disassociation of values, which is the gift of faith, from facts, the gift of intellect or reason. That is what makes reason and intellect sterile and unfit to be the sole guide of anyone to truth and life fulfillment.

THE *BUDDHI* OF VEDANTA AS WISDOM

Reason and intellect become creative when faith is integrated with them. This is the *buddhi* of Vedanta. *Buddhi* combines the creativity of *shraddha* with its sensitiveness to values, with the analytical power of the intellect with its grasp of facts, and adds also the power of pure will to itself. This is *buddhi* as the integral unity of faith-reason-will, evolved by humanity out of the neuropsychic energies given within by nature, and capable of leading an individual not only to discoveries in science, physical or spiritual, but also to the creation of great art, and to life fulfillment itself, both individual and collective.

It is, thus, obvious that the translation of *buddhi* as intellect severely limits its scope and meaning. Vedanta reveals its true form, when it presents *buddhi* as the faculty of luminous and creative and dynamic reason. It is highly eulogized in the *Upanishads* and the *Bhagavad Gita* [II.49]. The latter tells us "to put his or her life under its guidance."[19] *Buddhi* restores to the world and to human life the poetry and charm that was taken away by the intellect for its limited and specific handling of both. The *Katha Upanishad* [III.9] summons us to put the chariot of one's life under the guidance, not of the chariot, that is, the body, not of the horses, that is, the sensory system, not of the reins, the psychic system, but of the charioteer, one's *vijnana*, that is *buddhi*, or enlightened reason.

This conflict between reason and faith is overcome by the higher vision of a comprehensive spirituality of Indian philosophy. There were many people in India who swore by reason only, and there were other people in India who swore by faith only, and they both became narrow by that isolation and specialization. By the same token, there were plenty of people with emotionally held beliefs, weak of will, with no clear grasp of facts and often inclined to superstition and bigotry. But India's greatest teachers and books have always emphasized this harmonious combination of *shraddha* and *buddhi*, faith and reason, and also *dhrti*, will, to emerge as the instrument of a comprehensive spirituality encompassing the secular and the sacred, work and worship, as the luminous *buddhi*. Shankaracharya describes it as "*nedistham brahma*," closest to Brahman, closest to the innermost Self of all, the ultimate Reality in humanity and nature, ever present just behind the human psychic system. The ordinary reason or intellect is lit only by the feeble light of the senses and the sensory world in front, whereas the *buddhi* is lighted by the *ekam jyotisham jyotih*, "the one light of all lights,"—the Atman or Brahman, the light of pure Consciousness. It then becomes wisdom.

The philosophy of integral yoga of the *Bhagavad Gita* has this combination of knowledge (*jnana*), love of God (*bhakti*), meditation (*dhyana*), and dedicated action (*karma*). The clarity and grasp of facts of the trained intellect, the emotional richness of faith, and the dynamism of will, are unified in its *yoga* of *buddhi*. *Shraddha* without reason is blind; reason without *shraddha* is dry, sterile, and ineffective. That is why the *Bhagavad*

Gita and the *Srimad Bhagavatam* lay stress on the combination of *bhakti* and *jnana*. The latter exhorts us to practice love of God (*bhakti*), "combined with *jnana* and *vairagya*, knowledge and renunciation."[20] It is such *bhakti* that can penetrate into the heart of the mystery of God. This *bhakti* and how to cultivate it, and how innumerable devotees and saints and divine incarnations have expressed it in their lives, is the central theme of both of these books.

Thus, *jnana* (knowledge) needs *shraddha* (faith) and *shraddha* needs *jnana*. It is in this way that knowledge matures into wisdom. Otherwise, *jnana* alone would be dry intellectual knowledge, and *shraddha* blind belief or cheap sentimentalism. Our great spiritual teachers warn us often against that kind of one-sidedness.

If someone says, I *know* what love is, I have written a book on it and also have a doctorate in that subject, and you ask: have you experienced love, and he or she replies, "no," then what is the use of that voluminous knowledge? It is better to experience love, even a little of it, than merely knowing all the learned definitions about love. Facts or data of the sensory world are to be *known*; but values are to be *experienced*. When so experienced, values also become facts, but of a deeper world of experience.

This is why *jnana*, if it is mere intellectual knowledge, is respected though not respected greatly. It must have some other strength behind it, namely, intuition, the love of truth that culminates in wisdom. Therefore, says Krishna in the *Bhagavad Gita* [IV.40]: "The ignorant person, bereft also of *shraddha*, ever of a doubting nature, perishes." And, after stating "there is nothing equal to *jnana*, or knowledge," Krishna also affirms [IV.39]: "The one endowed with *shraddha* acquires *jnanam*." *Jnana* backed by *shraddha*, that *jnana* alone is radiant and redeeming.

THE VITAL ROLE OF IMAGINATION IN SCIENCE

As stated earlier, the scientist who wants to know the truth about nature must have a basic conviction that there is truth hidden in nature. With that conviction alone can he or she become a discoverer of the truths of nature. Otherwise the would-be scientist will remain a scientific scholar, who may quote scientific opinions on various subjects.

The sooner we realize this truth about science—that pure science is the product not only of a clear reason or a keen intellect, but also of some deep faith within the scientist, faith in oneself and in the truthfulness of nature, the better we shall understand the spirit of science and its close kinship with the other two disciplines in the pursuit of truth and human excellence, namely, art and religion, in which faith, in the form of imagination (*kalpana*), plays a greater role than reason.

Thus, apart from intellect or reason that functions in the discovery of truth in science, imagination also plays a vital part in all great scientific discoveries. As Max Planck has said in *Quantum Questions:* "The man who handles a bulk of results obtained from an experimental process must have an imaginative picture of the law that he is pursuing. . . . This imaginative vision and faith in the ultimate success are indispensable."[21] Imagination is what helps critical reason to develop into creative intuition. In the discovery of the universal truth of gravitation by Sir Isaac Newton, in the development of relativity and quantum theories in twentieth-century physics, in the discovery and demonstration of the unity of plants and animals and of the living and non-living by Sir J. C. Bose, and in several other instances, we can see this creative play of imagination, and its intuitive by-products, which are vital ingredients of *shraddha* or faith. Seeing an apple falling, Newton could make this inductive jump to the cosmic level: the same force of gravitation is what makes the moon fall toward the earth, what makes for the movements of all the planets and stars, and what reveals itself as a universal force exerted by every material body on other bodies in the universe.

Many scientists have highlighted this importance of imagination and resulting intuition as aids to critical reason in the discovery of scientific truths. Fritjof Capra, in his book, *The Tao of Physics* states:

> Rational knowledge and rational activities certainly constitute the major part of scientific research, but are not all there is to it. The rational part of research would, in fact, be useless if it were not complemented by the intuition that gives scientists new insights and makes them creative. These insights tend to come suddenly and, characteristically, not when sitting at a desk working out the equations, but when relaxing, in the bath, during a walk in the woods, on the beach, etc. During these periods of relaxation after concentrated intellectual activity, the intuitive mind seems to take over and can produce the sudden clarifying insights which give so much joy and delight to scientific research.[22]

The sense organs of cognition and the sense organs of action convert the animal body into a center of the most dynamic and varied activity in all nature. But at the level of the senses themselves, this activity is mostly uncoordinated and automatic and, therefore, not fit for purposes beyond mere physical survival. This coordination is achieved by nature in the human body in a new faculty of what neurologist Grey Walter calls "*imagination*" in his book *The Living Brain.*[23]

It is the capacity of the organism for imaging ideas and choosing from several alternatives before issuing forth in action in response to any sensory stimulus. It is this new capacity, which even the highest apes do not possess, says Grey Walter, that gave humanity dominance over nature and put it on the road to a new dimension of evolution itself, in continuation of organic evolution, namely, cultural evolution. He adds, with a touch of humor, that, if any one doubts the power of this new image-making faculty, let him consider the consequences of any other species than human beings developing this capacity; if the lion or the tiger or any other animal, for example, had developed this new faculty, we human beings would not have been here at all to discuss the subject!

Echoing the division of knowledge by ancient Indian philosophy into the subconscious and the unconscious of the dream and deep sleep states, into the conscious of the waking state, and the superconscious of the *samadhi* state, recent psychology suggests the addition of a third mode of cognition called "tertiary cognition" to the so far accepted two modes of cognition, namely, the primary cognition, standing for the subconscious or the preconscious in which imagination has full play, and the secondary cognition, standing for the conscious, or the rational in which the intellect has full play. This tertiary cognition combines within itself the creativity and spontaneity of the primary mode with the clarity and precision of the secondary mode.

In all these new developments of thought we can see a deeper and deeper understanding by modern humanity of the immense range and possibilities of the human mind long recognized in Indian thought. The finite mind can grasp only finite reality. The infinite reality can be realized only by the infinite mind. Purifying the mind, according to Vedanta, means eliminating its sensate limitations and its egoistic distortions. Sri Ramakrishna expresses a profound truth when he says that *shuddha manas*, pure mind, *shuddha buddhi*, pure reason, and *shuddha Atman*, pure Self, are one and the same truth.[24]

Imagination helps reason to discover new truths by induction from the known to the unknown. A scientist starts with some knowledge and says: this much I know, but what lies beyond it, I do not know; I feel it is there; my imagination tells me that there are deeper truths beyond what I have known and I shall continue my search for them. Here is seen the spirit of faith or *shraddha*, which has the strength to accommodate doubt as well, doubt of the creative kind. Similarly, when we come to the world of religion, we get the intimations that there are profound truths hidden beyond this perishable world revealed by the five senses, behind this perishable psychophysical organism and also the fleeting ego presiding over it which I call "myself."

We approach this profound mystery within human beings with the strength of this *shraddha*, but deepened and chastened by that earlier external investigation into the mystery of the physical universe, which every human being engages in, but scientists carry on more intensively. *Shraddha* in religion is the basic reverential attitude that the unknown, the unseen, the imperishable exists behind the known, the seen, the perishable. Reality as revealed by the five senses is so little; yet it is fascinating to the human mind.

How much more fascinating and rewarding must be the search and discovery of the reality that lies beyond the sensory level! All techniques of spiritual research and realization are to proceed on the strength of this basic *shraddha* with its ingredient of initial creative doubt as well. Such a research will be fruitless, it is obvious, if undertaken with an initial cynical attitude and its uncreative and sterile kind of doubt. That search does not exclude questioning. In Vedanta the approach to spiritual life is an integration of both reason and faith in order that anyone can question. There is some profound truth about humanity. We must realize that truth for ourselves. So the word *experience* travels along with faith in order to strengthen the scientific approach to religion.

"HAVE FAITH, O AMIABLE ONE"

In its scientifically and spiritually fascinating story of a long dialogue between Shvetaketu and his father Aruni, the *Chandogya Upanishad* highlights, in its exhortation: "*Shraddhasva, Somya,*" Have faith, O amiable one." There is a need for this type of *shraddha*, or creative faith when confronted by the mystery of the unknown behind the known.

The *Upanishad* introduces the dialogue with the story of the philosopher father sending his son, at the age of twelve, to the house of a guru for his education. The boy was returning home after his twelve-year education "while living in the guru's house." The father's question to his son on his welcome home, and the son's further education by the father, have great relevance to the needed re-shaping of education in our own time:

> Going to the teacher's house at the age of twelve years, he came back when he was twenty-four years old, having studied all the Vedas, conceited, arrogant, and regarding himself as very learned; marking this, his father said to him thus: "O Shvetaketu, I see you conceited, arrogant, and proud of your learning; but, O amiable one, did you ask from your teacher for that teaching about the One behind the many through which what is unheard becomes heard, what is unthought of becomes thought of, what is unknown becomes known?"
>
> "Of what nature, O revered one, is that teaching?" asked Shvetaketu.
>
> "Just as, O amiable one, through knowing a single clod of clay all that is made of clay will become known – all forms or modifications are

> merely names proceeding from words, and the knowledge that all is clay is alone true—such, indeed, O amiable one, is that teaching."
> "Surely, my revered teachers did not know this; for, if they had known, why should they not have told this to me? May your revered self alone tell (about) this to me."
> "Be it so, verily, O amiable one," said the father.[25]

Narrating the later part of the dialogue between the two, the *Upanishad* continues:

> "Please bring a fruit of the yonder banyan tree."
> "Here it is, O revered one."
> "Please break it."
> "It is broken, O revered one." "What do you find here?"
> "These atom-like grains, O revered one." "Please break one of these." "It is broken, O revered one." "What do you find here?"
> "Nothing whatsoever, O revered one."
> To him, the father said: "O amiable one, you do not see what is, verily, this atom-like (subtle part of the seed) yet, it is, verily, by this very atom-like (subtle essence) that this large banyan tree exists; *Shraddhasva*, Somya—have *shraddha*, O amiable one!"[26]

Bringing out the profound significance of the teacher's exhortation: *shraddhasva*, at this critical and delicate stage of the investigation, Shankaracharya says in his commentary on the passage:

> It is from that which is invisible and atom-like, and which is of the nature of *sat* (pure being), that the whole visible gross universe of effects, characterised by name and form etc., has come. Even though a truth established by scientific logic and scripture is accepted to be as such alone, even then, in the case of truths which are extremely subtle, there may be difficulty of comprehension, in the absence of a deeper faith, in the case of those minds that are *attached*, through natural propensities, to external objects; hence said the teacher: "have faith!" When such faith is present, there is the possibility of the mind calmly settling down on the truth that is sought after, in the wake of which will arise the grasp of its meaning.[27] [Italics added]

The above passages can well fit a student's approach to the comprehension of the "field" concept in modern physics. The field is that from which particles arise and into which they disappear. It is subtle and beyond sensory experience; and, in being no-thing, it is also everything.

To quote Frithjof Capra again:

> The field theories of modern physics force us to abandon the classical distinction between material particles and the Void. . . . In quantum

field theory, this field is seen as the basis of all particles and of their mutual interactions. . . .

. . . The vacuum is far from empty. On the contrary, it contains an unlimited number of particles which come into being and vanish without end.

Here, then, is the closest parallel to the Void of Eastern mysticism in modern physics. Like the Eastern Void, the "physical vacuum"—as it is called in field theory—is not a state of mere nothingness, but contains the potentiality for all forms of the particle world. These forms, in turn, are not independent physical entities but merely transient manifestations of the the underlying Void. . . .

The discovery of the dynamic quality of the vacuum is seen by many physicists as one of the most important findings of modern physics.[28]

The untrained human mind takes what is gross and what is experienced by the five senses as real, *sat*, or being. It considers what is subtle, and beyond the purview of the senses, as unreal, *asat*, or nonbeing. Standing at the final precipice of thought where all being melts into nonbeing, human thought needs to be fortified by creative and courageous faith to pursue truth whether it be in religion or in physical science. Whether it is in the realm of particle physics or of genetic biology, in respect of determining the true nature of life and of the individual—whether one is merely what is constituted of in the physical and chemical basis in the RNA and the DNA, or whether one has a higher dimension than these—scientific thought needs to be fortified by creative and courageous faith to pursue truth beyond the visible and tangible. It has to be recognized that what is considered to be nonbeing is really pure 'being' (*satyasya satyam*), the Truth of truth, in the light of which all energies, physical, biological, psychical, are also realized as true as the *Brhadaranyaka Upanishad* clearly expresses it:

Just as a spider (produces out of itself and) moves about in its own web, just as from a fire minute sparks fly about, exactly so, verily, from this Atman have come forth all (physical and biophysical and psychophysical) energies, all worlds, all gods, all beings. Its *Upanishad* ("mystic name") is Truth of truth. The energies, verily, are truth; this Atman is the Truth of those energies.[29]

The *Chandogya Upanishad*, in the words of the guru-father to his disciple-son, proclaims this *Truth of truth*, being of the nature of pure Consciousness, as the very Self of us all and the universe:

This, that which is the atom-like (subtle essence), this whole manifested universe has this as its self. That is the Truth. That is the Atman; and That thou art, O Shvetaketu![30]

REALITY AS *AKHANDA SAT-CHIT-ANANDA*/ INDIVISIBLE BEING, CONSCIOUSNESS, BLISS

In particle physics, the characterization of subatomic hadron reactions as a flow of energy in which particles are continually created and dissolved, and the description of the extremely short-lived hadron states as resonances, suggest more an *event* than a material object, and echo the Hindu vision of the universe at its deeper levels as consisting of *sphota*, that is, sound. This raises the question of the nature of these *events*.

Modern physics has been in search of the true nature of matter. At and above the atomic level, we come across its stable atomic and molecular structural forms making up our normal physical universe of human sensory experience. Below the atomic level, physics comes across all matter in the form of energies, the description of which becomes appropriate only when done in relativistic and quantum terms. This means, as remarked by Sir James Jeans, seeing nature after removing our human spectacles.

As pellets of energies, the hadrons and resonances are still matter. The search for the elementary state of matter has traveled a long distance from the atoms (later designated as molecules) of early Greek philosophers, through the atoms of classical physics, to particles and the quantum field, and now to the resonances, of twentieth-century physics. What keenness of intellect and what depth of faith were present in these scientific quests!

It is interesting to note, from the point of view of Vedanta, that some particle physicists today raise the question not only as to whether these elementary particles are really structureless and therefore truly elementary, but also whether there can be elementary particles at all in view of their participation in the interaction process, which implies, according to Fritjof Capra:

> . . . the important conclusion that the known particles must have some internal structure, because only then can they interact with the observer and thus be detected.[31]

That a particle must possess internal structure otherwise it could not be detected has been voiced also by Geoffrey Chew in his book *Great Ideas Today*.[32] Vedanta finds an echo in this observation for it discovered ages ago that structurelessness, indivisibility, *cannot* be found as the characteristic, not only of matter and energy, including the quarks, but also of time and space, and even of the four-dimensional space-time, and that anything and everything that possesses internal structure are unreal, (*mithya*), because they are all *objects* of knowledge, or observation (*drshyam*), in the technical language of Vedanta, because they are also *pratiksanam anyatha svabhavah*, "of a changing nature from moment to moment," as observed by Shankaracharya. As if in anticipation of Heisenberg's Uncertainty Principle, Sri Ramakrishna remarked in 1884, "There is much confusion in this world of His *maya*. One can by no means say that 'this' will come after 'that' of 'this' will produce 'that'."[33]

Vedanta, therefore, sought in its *paravidya*, higher science, which the *Mundaka Upanishad* [I.1.5] defines as "that science by which the imperishable (dimension of reality) is realized," for that structureless and indivisible reality in the seer or the observer (the *drk*), of which these are merely passing configurations, possessing only separate names and forms, as expressed by the *Chandogya Upanishad* quoted earlier. In such *Upanishads* as the *Taittiriya* [II.7.1] Vedanta discovered the seer to be pure Consciousness, and discovered also the unity of all seers and the seen, of the separate and diverse phenomena of the material world outside, and all manifestation of consciousness centered in the egos of the individual seers within. It proclaimed that pure Consciousness alone is and can be indivisible, or truly elementary. Vedanta terms it the *akhanda sat-chit-ananda*, undivided Existence-Consciousness-Bliss, or as some would say, Indivisible Being, Consciousness, Bliss.

"It has been revealed to me, said Sri Ramakrishna, "that there exists an Ocean of Consciousness without limit. From It come all things of the relative plane, and in It they merge again."[34]

The indivisible *sat-chit-ananda* is the "Light of all lights." It is the impersonal-personal God of Vedanta, both of its philosophy and of its religion. The philosopher reasons and discriminates between the abiding and the fleeting, stresses its impersonal and formless aspect, while the devotee full of faith and devotion stresses its personal aspect with form. This form is the condensation of the same divine ocean of pure Consciousness due to the cooling influence of love of God, says Sri Ramakrishna. In Vedantic devotional meditation the devotee meditates in the heart, conceived as a full-blown lotus, the radiant divine form condensed out of the Infinite Light and later dissolving into it at the end of meditation. The lotus, in Indian culture and art, is the symbol of regeneration. Many are the symbols in all the cultures and religions in the world.

Ekam sat, vipra bahudha vadanti: "Truth is one.[35] Sages call it by various names," proclaims the ancient *Rig-Veda*. *Yato mat tato path*: "As many religions, so many pathways to God,"[36] proclaims Sri Ramakrishna in our own time.

It is this comprehension of divine unity that made Vedanta inspire India with the vision and practice of active tolerance and harmony, not only between different religions, but also between religion and science, faith and reason, religion and secular thought and practice. The *Srimad Bhagavatam* proclaims this supreme truth, *tattvam*, (different from personal preference or opinion, *matam*), of an all-comprehending unity in one of its famous verses:

> Knowers of the Supreme Truth, (*tattvam*), declare that it is one and the same nondual pure Consciousness that is spoken of as Brahman, or the impersonal Absolute (by the philosohers), as *Paramatman*, or the supreme Self (by the mystics), and as *Bhagavan*, or the all-loving God by the devotees.[37]

The philosopher stresses the Being and Consciousness aspects of the Supreme Truth and the devotee stresses these and its bliss aspect in addition. It is this bliss aspect that inspires all art also.

The *Upanishads* further emphasize this aesthetic component of the ultimate Reality by saying:

> He (Brahman) is, verily, *rasa* (i. e. bliss or delight); this (living being) experiences bliss (in life) by getting (a bit of) this *rasa*.[38]

The *Bhagavad Gita* presents this truth of the nature of pure Consciousness, one and non-dual, and the truth of all matter and energy and all individual centers of consciousness of the universe as its configurations, in five great verses:

> (It is) without and within (all) beings, both unmoving and moving; because It is subtle, It is incomprehensible: It is far as well as near.
>
> Itself undivided, it exists in all divided things as if divided; it should also be known as the sustainer of all things, as well as their absorber and creator.
>
> It is the Light of all lights, beyond all darkness (of ignorance and delusion): (as the one Self in all, It is) knowledge, object of knowledge, and the goal of knowledge, (ever) established in the heart of all.
>
> He sees (indeed), who sees (the one) supreme Lord existing equally (or integrally) in all beings, imperishable in things that perish.
>
> When one realizes all separately existing things and beings as existing in the One, and their expansion from That (One) only, then one attains Brahman.[39]

Nuclear physicist Erwin Schroedinger in his book, *What is Life?* reflects this Vedantic truth of *atmaikatva-vidya pratipattaye sarve Vedantah arabhyante* – "the unity of the Atman as Pure Consciousness which is the goal of all the Upanishads," as expressed by Shankaracharya in his *Brahma-Sutras* commentary on Sutra 4:

> Consciousness is never experienced in the plural, only in the singular. Consciousness is a singular of which the plural is unknown; that there

> *is* only one thing, and that what seems to be a plurality is merely a series of different aspects of this one thing, produced by a deception (the Indian *maya*).[40]

DRG-DRSHYA-VIVEKA DISCRIMINATION BETWEEN OBSERVER AND OBSERVED

The quantum energy-field or the four-dimensional space-time, which physics presents as beyond sensory verification, finds its counterpart in Vedanta in its *chittakasha*, the *akasha* or the Void, of *chitta* or mind. This is the knowledge-field or Consciousness-field, of which the seer and the seen, the observer and the observed, are but two poles. By *drg-drshya-viveka*, is meant the discrimination between the seer and the seen, or the observer and the observed, leading to a knowledge of their unity.

This Vedantic truth will become revealed to subatomic physics when it resolves its present contradiction involved in viewing its "observer" in terms of classical physics while viewing its "observed" in terms of quantum probabilities.

Vedanta speaks of mind and matter as the subtle and gross forms of one and the same reality. Hence, it was never obsessed, as Western thought was and still is, with the mind-body conflict or the mind-matter conflict. Being the subtle aspect of matter, mind is not a tangible reality such as are matter and the physical world.

It is about this *chitta* or mind that the great neurologist Sir Charles Sherrington said, from the point of view of modern neurology, that "it remains without sensual confirmation, and it remains without it forever."[41] What he said about mind is exactly what the great mathematician-physicist Eddington said about matter from the point of view of modern physics. Eddington also maintained: "But no one can deny that mind is the first and most direct thing in our experience, and all else is remote inference . . . .[42]

To come back to the field of the mind or *chittakasha*; it still involves the duality of the seer and the seen, the observer and the observed, and therefore provokes a deeper inquiry. This duality is finally overcome in the "field of pure Consciousness," the *chidakasha*, which is the same field of the mind viewed *noncasually*. Vedanta describes the search for, and the discovery of, the true observer, the Self, in two famous verses of the *Drg-drshya-Viveka*, a treatise on the inquiry into discrimination between the observer (*Drg*) and the observed (*Drshya*):

> When form is the object of observation or *drshyam*, then the eye is the observer or *drk*; when the eye is the object of observation, then the mind is the observer; when the pulsations of the mind are the objects of observation, then the *Sakshi* or the Witness-Self is the real observer; and it is always the observer and, being self-luminous, can never be the object of observation.

> When the notion and the attachment that one is the physical body is dissolved, and the supreme Self is realised, wherever the mind goes, (there) one experiences *samadhi*.[43]

By thus presenting the universe in its fundamental aspect as pure Consciousness only, Vedanta does not destroy the universe or its matter, but only *illumines* the true nature of both, just as modern quantum and relativity physics do not destroy the stable molecular structures of the physical world by presenting that world as an ocean of energy, but maintain that the stable familiar world presented by classical physics is only a *limiting* case of the world presented by quantum and relativity physics. Knowledge does not destroy or create, it only illumines, *jnapakam hi sastram, na karakam, iti sthitih,* says Shankaracharya.[44]

In his talks and discussions with Reneé Weber, professor of philosophy at Rutgers University, the theoretical physicist David Bohm has deepened and enlarged his thinking on consciousness. From "Rather consciousness is a material process" and "Consciousness is possibly a more subtle form of matter and movement,[45] Bohm and Reneé Weber in a dialogue printed in *Quantum Implications* (1987) reflect on consciousness:

> Weber: "You are more and more interested in meaning, so can we explore what meaning is; not the definitive essence of it, but why are you interested in it?"
>
> Bohm: "I am interested in meaning because it is the essential feature of consciousness, because meaning is being as far as the mind is concerned."
>
> Weber: "*Is* meaning being?"
>
> Bohm: "Yes. A change of meaning is a change of being. If we say consciousness is its content, therefore consciousness is meaning. We could widen this to a more general kind of meaning that may be the essence of all matter as meaning."[46]

And towards the end of the dialogue:

> Weber: "You are really saying *our being is meaning*. The whole world *is* meaning."
>
> Bohm: "Yes. The being of matter is its meaning: the being of ourselves is meaning: the being of society is its meaning. The mechanistic view has created a rather crude and gross meaning which has created a crude and gross and confused society."[47]

If meaning were not enfolded in consciousness, life would be meaningless.

The material universe of daily experience, which physics sets about to study, will reveal its true form as pure Consciousness, when physics dissociates the "matter," which it studies, from the dogma of "materialism" that it wrongly associates with it. Materialism is an *intruder* in physical science, while matter is a useful working concept for it,[48] according to Thomas Huxley.

The physical universe we see and know but never experience; consciousness we experience but never see and know in that way. Vedanta, as philosophy, combines knowledge with experience. That is the meaning of Wisdom. The charge of many Western thinkers that Vedanta is not a philosophy but a religion is true from this point of view. Certainly, Vedanta is not mere speculative philosophy relying simply on logical reason. The limitation of logical reason is also admitted by scientists and rationalists today. Vedanta emphasizes the need for the *experience* of Reality, which gives it its religious character as well. It is *tattva-darshan*, experience of Truth.

Vedanta sees the limitations of speculative reason as arising from its exclusive confinement to, and being conditiond by, the experience of the waking-state. That reveals only the not-self aspect of reality, the segment of reality studied by both Western philosophy and classical physics. But Western depth psychology and twentieth-century physics have touched a subtler dimension of reality, the self-aspect, the segment revealed in the dream-state. Dreams reveal the unity of the seer, *drk*, and the seen, *drshyam*, as the one mind-stuff, but not while dreaming, when the sharp diversities of the waking-state continue to be experienced, but only on waking. In *susupti*, the deep sleep-state, all objects, *drshyam*, disappear altogether into the Void as the unity of all objects, of all waking and dream presentations. When viewed non-casually, this is the supreme truth of the Atman; and this is realized in a new waking-state, called "*turiya*," the fourth, or the transcendental state.

In order to understand or realize the true nature of *turiya* and not merely to speculate about it, one needs the *strength of purest faith* along with the strength of clearest reason. At this deeper level, faith and reason, pure religion and pure science, come together. And both are needed for the fullest comprehension of truth as well as for total life fulfillment. In the words of Capra:

> The modern physicist experiences the world through an extreme specialization of the rational mind; the mystic through an extreme specialization of the intuitive mind. The two approaches are entirely different and involve far more than a certain view of the physical world. However, they are complementary, as we have learned to say in physics. Neither is comprehended in the other, nor can either of them be reduced to the other, but both of them are necessary, supplementing one another for

> a fuller understanding of the world. To paraphrase an old Chinese saying, mystics understand the roots of the Tao but not its branches; scientists understand its branches but not its roots. Science does not need mysticism and mysticism does not need science; but man needs both.[49]

There is another consideration with regard to the validity and fruitfulness of such faith in the unseen, so far as religion is concerned. There have been, and there are, people who have gone beyond this world of the senses and discovered the Atman, the Self, and God, the one Self of all. "This *nirvikalpa*, the transcendental state, has been realized, the nondual (reality) in which the ever changing universe is dissolved," as the *Mandukya Karika* testifies in verse [II, 35]. People have realized truths which, in the terminology of Vedanta and Buddhism, are transcendent (*lokottara*), beyond the *loka* or the sense world or relativity and impermanence. The records of these realizations, moreover, are available to the rest of humanity in texts like the *Upanishads* in India, and similar texts in other countries and cultures.

When anyone proceeds on this quest, he or she has two such sources of strength behind him or her. First, a general sense of the meaningfulness of the universe; that behind this organic existence and the environing sensory world there are profound truths waiting to be explored. And, second, the knowledge that the transcendental field of experience has been already explored by hundreds of competent people, men and women, and the insights gained by them are available for the guidance of the rest of humanity.

The beginner on this strange path, this challenging *terra incognita*, has something to rely upon in the insights gained by such pioneers in the spiritual path, who are truthful and trustworthy, and who, furthermore, do not on their part ask the rest of us to blindly believe and follow them but to use their discoveries as starting points, and to experiment and recheck the discoveries ourselves. This is the meaning and significance of the Hindu idea of the greatness and relevance of the *shruti*, or the *Upanishads*, as *apta vakya*, words of competent persons.

About the value and limitation of all the holy books of humanity, Sri Ramakrishna muses in one of his parables: The Vedas, the Bible, the Koran, and other sacred books of religions *do not contain truth or God*; they contain only *information* about truth or God. One must use that information to find Truth or God for himself or herself. Sri Ramakrishna concludes: "Books, scriptures, and things like that only point the way to reach God. . . . But after getting all the information about the path, you must begin to work."[50]

Such is the place of *shraddha* in spiritual life. Thus, we come to the example of Sri Ramakrishna, who began with doubt and questioning when he started his spiritual quest as a worshipper in the Kali temple of Dakshineswar. Sitting before the image in the temple, worshipping and praying to the Mother to reveal Her pure Consciousness form, Sri Ramakrishna would plead:

> Art Thou true, Mother, or is it all fiction – mere poetry without any reality? If Thou dost exist, why do I not see Thee. Is religion a mere fantasy and art Thou only a figment of man's imagination?[51]

This creative *shraddha* with its clear and pure imagination fortified by an overpowering love of truth and the dynamic disciplines undergone in its search, gave to the modern world an extraordinary scientist in the world of religion in Sri Ramakrishna.

In this approach to religion by Sri Ramakrishna – and this is the authentic tradition of religion in India, from the *Upanishads* through Buddha, to modern times – we can see the coexistence of a luminous *shraddha* with doubt, a rational questing, and a questioning mind. His *shraddha* did not silence doubt but quickened it and made it creative. This is also the role of doubt in all the physical sciences and explains the Indian spiritual tradition's kinship with, and hospitality toward, modern physical science.

THE WILL TO BELIEVE, FAITH AND PERSEVERANCE

Doubt based on *shraddha* is creative. Such doubt is wholesome and necessary, but mere doubt, and too much of it, is bad. If too much of "the will to believe" is bad, too much of "the will to doubt and disbelieve" is equally so. Many of our contemporaries have this "will to disbelieve" to an unhealthy degree, just as many of our traditionalists have the "will to believe" in the same measure. The extreme form of the former is what was referred to earlier as cynicism, as the extreme of the latter is what is described as gullibility.

Cynicism of this kind, that is, of the "will to disbelieve" signifies spiritual death. No new truth can be discovered by a person of that type, no value can such a one ever experience in life. The very impulse to seek, and the spirit of *shraddha* behind it, are the very lifeblood of science and religion. In the words of Sir Arthur Eddington:

> You can neither understand the spirit of true science, nor of true religion, unless you keep seeking in the forefront.[52]

Sri Ramakrishna expounds this truth, and the meditation technique of all religions, through the illustration of fishing. What do we do when we want to catch a fish? We take a fishing rod and line, fix an attractive bait to its hook, go to a lake, and cast the line with the bait into the lake. We then sit calmly, watching. We may not have actually seen any fish in the lake, but we have the basic faith that there are fish in the lake, having heard that others have caught fish there. Sometimes, we may have to sit there for a long time. After an hour or two, if we fail to catch any fish, we won't conclude that there aren't any fish in the lake. We will heed the exhortation of the *Upanishad* referred to earlier, "Have faith, O amiable one" (*shraddhasva somya*), and come again the next day and again the day after. We may not have caught any fish, but we continue our effort. What is it that sustains our dogged efforts? It is a basic belief that the lake does contain fish. This basic faith is further strengthened by the knowledge that others had come before us and had succeeded in their efforts in catching fish. That means that there are fish in the lake, though we ourselves have not discovered any yet, and that we shall also have success if we persist and persevere. This positive attitude, and action inspired by that attitude, is behind all discoveries of truth in physical sciences and religion.

The sages of the *Upanishads* belong to this category. Day after day, year after year, they persisted in their search for the truth of the human soul, for the truth of God. They faced every possible obstacle, disciplined their senses, calmed their minds, concentrated the energies of both and made them penetrate into the inner world, and then discovered to their joy, and to the joy and welfare of the rest of humanity, the universal spiritual truths that have reached us through Vedanta and Buddhism.

To continue Sri Ramakrishna's parable of fishing. After long watching, we see the float trembling. This is the visible sign from which we get the intimation about the invisible happenings below, that surely a fish is nibbling at the bait below. But soon it goes away, leaving us waiting and watching, but strengthened in our initial *shraddha*. And the next time we watch the float tremble, we feel a pull at the rod and conclude that a large fish has swallowed the bait. We pull up the line and hook, and up comes the fish into our hands! In spiritual life, the bait that we fix to the hook of our mind is love of God and purity of character and sincerity in our search for God, which alone can attract God.

Describing this arduous technique of the pioneering sages, which yielded as its sweet fruit the preeminent science of spirituality, Yama, the teacher, tells young Nachiketas, the student, in a compressed verse of the *Katha Upanishad*:

> The self-existent (Reality) constructed the sense organs of man with the initial defect of an outgoing disposition; therefore (humanity) sees (i. e.,

> experiences) the external world, but not the inner Self. A certain heroic seeker turned (the energies of) the senses (and of the mind) inward, with the desire to attain immortality, and realized the (one divine) inner Self.[53]

The search for truth in the sciences involves similar challenges, setbacks, and disappointments; it calls for similar courage and persistence to achieve the end. Behind a successful scientific discovery lie many failures and disappointments. Take the case of Madame Curie who discovered and isolated radium. Behind that momentous discovery lay years of frustrating research with pitchblende, conducted in a damp and ill-equipped cellar, and in a spirit of what India calls *"tapas,"* or austere discipline in the pursuit of truth, in which she had the help and encouragement of her great scientist husband. Thus, we see the close kinship in method and spirit and temper between the austere discipline of physical science and the science of religion. Gaudapada, a Vedantic teacher of the seventh century A.D., refers to the dauntless persistence characteristic of all such austerity (*tapas*) in a famous verse in his *Mandukya Karika*:

> The disciplining of the mind is to be pursued with dauntless and cheerful determination just like the determination to empty the ocean, drop by drop, by the tip of a *Kusha* grass.[54]

The spirit behind both pure science and religion, therefore, is the same, namely, persistent search for truth; the difference lies only in the field of the search. The physical scientists have been seeking for truth in the physical universe, in the world revealed by the five senses, and by instruments helpful to the senses. The seeker of the science of religion seeks for it in that field of experience that lies beyond the world revealed by the five senses, beyond "where the organ of speech (and other senses) and the mind (dependent on mere sense data), do not reach," as the *Taittiriya Upanishad*[55] puts it. Soul and God belong to that category. That is India's testament after long experiments and verifications, from the time of the *Upanishads* to Sri Ramakrishna.

That is why, in the field of religion in India, the question is not of believing in a creed or dogma, but experimenting with and experiencing the truth about the soul, about God. Gandhi's autobiography is entitled *The Story of My Experiments With Truth*. He wrote: "But I should certainly like to narrate my experiments in the spiritual field which are known only to myself, and from which I have derived such power as I possess for working in the political field."[56] Gandhi, a householder, became Mahatma Gandhi, a great soul, an outstanding example of *karma-yoga*.

Belief is nothing. As was said in the beginning, any fool can say "I believe" and he or she believes; yet he or she remains the same stagnant pool of a man or a woman for years and years. That belief has not made any difference in his or her character, or in his or her personal and professional interhuman relationships.

But one who follows the way of the science of religion does not remain satisfied with such a smug belief yielding only a static piety. Such a one dares to question his or her own belief, to experiment with it, and does not find satisfaction until it has been found to be a true belief. Indian history is full of accounts of spiritual seekers, drawn from all classes and levels of society, who evolved and became saints – scientific discoverers in the field of religion.

Incidentally, it also demonstrates the truth that the scientific mind and the spiritual mind, in a free society, can rise and flourish irrespective of caste, class, education, or income level. Those saints meditated and prayed, struggled and suffered, lived and worked with dedication for years before they experienced the light of God. The discoveries of physical science have also such *tapas* (austerity) behind them, as the one example out of many, that of Madame Currie mentioned earlier, makes clear. The training of all, including children to have a scientific attitude, will in due course fit them for pure religion also. Search for truth in all of science begins with the sense organs by transforming *mere seeing* into *observing*. The training of the senses and the mind into effective instruments in the search for truth and character is education. Religion is but education continued.

It was the act of observing that played a great part in the eventual development of the steam engine. When James Watts [1736–1819] was a young boy, he was sitting at the breakfast table with other members of his family. His mother was preparing the breakfast. The kettle, filled with water for tea, was on the fire and the water was boiling. The boy looked at the kettle. He saw the lid on the kettle jumping up. He *observed* it, not merely saw it, and felt it to be a unique phenomenon. The mother called the boy to join the party at breakfast, but he did not hear it: he was so absorbed in that one single phenomenon in front of him, and in the course of observation his mind caught its significance imaginatively: there is power, or energy, hidden in the steam. It makes the lid jump up all the time, and that energy can be made to serve the purposes of humanity. Out of that experience came the great discovery of the steam engine, which was one of the important ingredients of the early phase of the Industrial Revolution.

In another such youth of India, the late Dr. Yallapragada Subba Row of Andhra Pradesh, we have a wonderful recent example of perseverance in a scientific quest. When I read his story in the *American Reporter* of

New Delhi[57] I felt not only deeply inspired, but also that there is a need to awaken the *Subba Row spirit*, consisting of love of truth and the inquiring spirit, and also love of people, in many millions of today's youths. What did he do? As a student at school at Madras, he was a bright boy, but very poor. His brother fell ill of sprue of a serious kind. The boy watched his brother sinking day by day from what, at that time, was an incurable malady. Helplessly watching the dear brother dying away, his imagination became fired with the thought: Why is my brother dying like this? Is there no remedy for this serious ailment? And he then and there resolved within himself that he would dedicate his life to finding such a remedy, which he did. This story illustrates the confluence of self-discipline or *tapas* and study-research or *svadhyaya*, highly praised and prized in Valmiki's *Ramayana* and other great books of Indian culture.

What a resolution for a young and poor school boy to make! But when behind such resolutions lie love of truth and love of humanity and courage, they cease to be idle resolutions of immature minds, but become creative movements of the human soul pressing silently on. Love of truth and love of humanity go together in many scientific and spiritual discoveries, as also in many social undertakings like prison reform, in the medical field, in surgery, therapeutics and preventive medicine. Buddha's compassion for human beings made him discover profound spiritual truths during his historic meditation under the Bodhi Tree at Buddha Gaya two thousand five hundred years ago. Gandhi's going to prison, armed with truth and nonviolence only, was with a view to releasing millions of his countrymen from the larger prison of political slavery and helplessness.

After his matriculation, young Subba Row was helped by friends to study medicine. He duly finished the M.B.B.S. and M.S. courses. But, all through his schooling only one idea dominated his mind: How to discover a remedy for that pernicious ailment. So, after finishing his medical course at Madras, he wanted to do research. But where were such research facilities in India then? So he traveled first to the United Kingdom in 1923 and afterwards to America where he joined a research team at Harvard University. Along with doing commendable research work there, he also worked diligently and obtained a degree in biochemistry. During this time, in order to meet his expenses, he did some menial jobs to earn enough money. He later accepted an invitation, extended by the Lederle Laboratories of the American Cyanimid Company, New York, in 1940, to use its facilities for his research. Impressed with his earnestness and talents, the management of that drug research laboratory encouraged him to go ahead in his search and, from 1942, to direct the research work of its team of scientists.

Research with tons of liver for experiment continued for years. Like many other scientific seekers, he, too, must have often experienced frustration and dejection; the expected results were not always forthcoming. Ultimately, he succeeded in isolating a tiny bit of folic acid in the form of a yellow powder in 1945. It was a great discovery. Then came its testing by application to hospital patients. When it was administered, the results were marvelous, and it soon entered the market as a wonderful remedy for the pernicious tropical disease of sprue.

Subba Row did not take any personal credit for this discovery, but he gave credit to the members of his team. Soon after, he and his team developed another wonder drug: Aureomycin. During all those years he gave freely from his earnings to relieve the sufferings of other people around him. Dr. Yellapragada Subba Row died in the United States in 1948 at the young age of 52. He ensured, through his work, life for millions of his fellow human beings.

The Lederle Laboratories have honored his memory with the installation of his bust in their laboratory at Bulsar, Gujarat State, India, below which is a description of him as scientist, teacher, philosopher, humanitarian, and followed by the inscription: Science Simply Prolongs Life; Religion Deepens It.

His life illustrates the spirit conveyed in a brief but powerful utterance by queen mother Vidula to her prince son Sanjaya, as recorded in the *Udyogaparva* of the *Mahabharata*:

> *Muhurtam jvalitam shreyo, na tu dhumayitam chiram:* It is better to flame forth for one instant than to smoke away for ages![58]

DYNAMIC SPIRITUALITY

As taught by the *Bhagavad Gita*, the true devotee, or seeker of God, is one who combines within oneself clear thinking, rich emotions and imagination, and strong will. That is the profound teaching of the *Sanatana Dharma*, or Eternal Religion, of India. Any and every foolish belief and superstition is not part of religion. Believing in all sorts of fairy tales, legends, and stories, which have no human reference or moral and spiritual appeal, is not part of religion, neither is believing in cheap magic and miracles.

In the long evolutionary process in the science of spirituality, one transcends the Scriptures with their do's and don'ts and all these static traditions. When one experiences the truth for oneself, then one alone attains to the knowledge of God, knowledge of the imperishable Reality, the *akshara*, which is the subject of *paravidya*, wisdom. Knowledge rising to wisdom is only when one begins to *experience* the profound truth about oneself, that behind and beyond these passing configurations of psycho-physical individuality, one realizes the one infinite imperishable Atman.

In all scientific investigations into the human inner dimension, which is also the inner dimension of nature—for humans are nature's finest product of evolution—all knowing tends to be 'being'; to know it, is to *be* it. In no physical science is this true. If one knows the table, one doesn't become the table. When one knows the sun, one doesn't become the sun. But in the science of the inner nature of humanity, when one knows the Atman, one becomes the Atman, one's divine nature. When one knows God, one becomes God, or becomes God-like. What a beautiful idea! Here one finds speculative knowledge becoming experiential knowledge; this is what Vedanta calls "knowledge maturing into wisdom."

All science is the search for the imperishable behind the perishable, for the absolute behind the relative. What is the imperishable? Everything in the universe is perishable. The whole galactic system is perishable. So are our own bodies. Only through the pursuit of Truth into the depth level of experience, says Vedanta, will one get the imperishable and the immortal. One realizes oneself as truly the immortal. I am not this body. I am the Self. That wonderful knowledge is not secondhand knowledge, but firsthand or direct experience. But this search must have faith behind it. Otherwise the intellect becomes drab and dry.

How can these eyes show the eternal Atman or the infinite Brahman? How can these ears manifest it? None of the sense organs, nor the mind held in captivity by the sense organs, can reveal it. But the mind that has become pure and concentrated, that has unified within itself pure imagination, pure intelligence, and pure will, becomes *buddhi*. This *buddhi*, then, can penetrate into the heart of Truth as expounded by Yama to Nachiketas in the *Katha Upanishad*:

> Superior to the sense organs is *manas* (mind); more excellent than *manas* is *buddhi* (reason); higher than *buddhi* is *mahat* (the cosmic mind); higher than *mahat* is *avyakta* (nature in its undifferentiated state).
>
> Superior even to *avyakta* is the *Purusha* (the Self), all-pervading and entirely devoid of any particularising indicative mark, knowing Whom every creaturely individual is emancipated and attains immortality.
>
> His form is not within the field of sight, none can see him with the (physical) eye; He is revealed in (the Void of) the heart by the *manas* that is fully under the control of the *buddhi*. Those who realise this become immortal.[59]

Cut open the physical body and examine it. Can you see the Atman there? Not at all; for it is the Self and not the non-Self; it is the seer, the observer, and not the seen, the observed. Physical science has no relevance there; its work will end in the field of pure science when it lands the human seeker on the shores of the unknown but ever present *drk* or the seer at the end of the voyage of discovery of the world of the *drshyam* or the seen. Atman is seen, says the last verse quoted from the *Katha Upanishad* [VI.9], by a penetrating vision, the product of a converging life endeavor based on moral character together with the concentration and the turning inward of the energies of the senses and the mind.

Indian tradition emphasizes the fact that *shruti,* meaning the *Upanishads,* has no authority in the sensate field of experience. In that field, researchers and students must follow the authority of the physical sciences, which are also *vastu-tantra-jnana,* knowledge based on the existing reality, of the sensory level of experience. So when the body is sick, help is sought from the physical science of medicine, which may be modern allopathy, yoga-aided psychiatry, homeopathy, nature cure, or ancient Indian *ayurveda.* It would be foolish to go to quacks and religious magicians to find a cure.

But when the ailments are spiritual, arising from what the Hindu tradition characterizes as the *shad-ripus,* or "six enemies," namely, *kama,* or lust, *krodha,* or anger, *lobha,* or greed, *moha,* or delusion, *mada,* or pride, and *matsarya,* or violence and conflict, it is advisable to turn to the science of spirituality for help. It is this science of spirituality that can help prevent the fears that are assailing many people today. These fears, arising from the human inner nature, are creating psychic distortions in people, which manifest themselves as anxiety, tension, frustration, boredom, as well as violence, crime, and even inclination to suicide. These are all the evil fruits of psychic distortions within humanity, even though our physical sciences have brought order and richness in human outer life. For the production of love and kindness, compassion and dedication, peace and fulfillment, one must resort to the science of the inner life, which is religion.

In the field of the science of religion, one takes leave of the sense organs, the sensate mind, and the world revealed by them. Meditation is the unique technique of the science of spirituality. The first thing one does during meditation is to abandon the sense organs and the sensate mind, for they are of no use to us there, because we are not then in search of the reality revealed by the sense organs. If that reality alone existed, there would be no meaning in closing our eyes or other sense organs, and calming our minds; in fact we would rather keep them wide open and scatter their energies outside, which is exactly what we are doing in our so-called 'normal' worldly life. But we feel that a deeper, vaster, and more meaningful dimension of reality, and of our own personality, waits for us beyond the sensate level. To get in touch with it we feel the need to "discipline the senses" and to "calm the mind," two processes known as *"dama"* and *"shama"* in the Hindu tradition. They are the mental counterparts of the physical homeostasis achieved by nature for us in the long course of organic evolution.

Going into the depths of one's self, the more wide and comprehensive become one's understanding and sympathy. The more inward one goes, the more widespreading in range and depth becomes one's capacity to communicate affection to other people. Thus, one breaks down barriers to neighborliness. At the circumference of the circle, all the radii are different. These differences diminish as one proceeds toward the center, and completely vanish when one reaches the center from where one can have direct and spontaneous connection with any point at the circumference.

All spiritual growth is a movement toward that one center where all objects and subjects meet and that is the idea of God in Vedanta. The following definition of God and man was given by Swami Vivekananda in the San Francisco area in 1900: The soul is a circle of which the circumference is nowhere, but the center is in the body. God is a circle whose circumference is nowhere, but whose center is everywhere![60]

All spiritual growth gives one increasing spiritual energy resources, which is the growth that humanity needs today to deal successfully with the enormous human distortions in our civilization.

It appears that modern physical science is on the brink of a productive confrontation with the new datum of mind and consciousness, which is evident in nuclear physics itself. Twentieth-century biology presents it, similarly, in its stress on organic evolution rising, at the human stage, to the higher level of psychosocial evolution. Other scientific writers of the post-WWII years also refer to this exciting possibility. One such is contained in an article on "Aspects of an Upheavel in Medicine" by H. Schipperges, which appeared in Sieman's *Electromedica*:

> Scarcely have we discovered the cosmos and are behind the moon, when there awaits us a new universe, namely, the full inside of nature, the kingdom of the "soul", as it was previously called, the dimension of depth, that "in the inside there is also a universe" as Goethe said, actually a multiverse, the perspective of our modern world which nowhere shows *the* world, but worlds, situations, anthropologies, fragments, aspects in upheavel. Everything in this grandiose, hectic, and also moving panorama of the ending second millenium points to the conclusion that we are in the middle of a second enlightenment.[61]

As mentioned earlier, Sir Charles Sherrington had referred to this mystery of mind and consciousness, haunting his subject of neurology, during his Gifford lectures on natural theology without reference to creed held in Edinburgh at the university on *Man on His Nature*:

> Mind, for anything perception can compass, goes therefore in our special world more ghostly than a ghost. Invisible, intangible, it is a thing not even of outline; it is not a "thing." It remains without sensual confirmation and it remains without it forever.[62]

Alongside this it is interesting to read what Sir Arthur Eddington said about the like mystery of "matter" in the introduction to his Gifford lecture on *The Nature of the Physical World:*

> . . . In the world of physics, we watch a shadowgraph performance of the drama of familiar life. The shadow of my elbow rests on the shadow table as the shadow ink flows over the shadow paper. . . . The frank realization that physical science is concerned with a world of shadows is one of the most significant of recent advances.[63]

In the light of such inner penetration achieved by Vedanta, India's testament is that, whether it is physical science or the science of religion, *shraddha*, faith, and *buddhi*, reason, need to cooperate with each other, and that they never conflict with each other, if the search is for truth and human fulfillment. The more one strengthens one's reason, the better one's religious life. Any foolish and temporary emotion, is not devotion to God (*bhakti*). *Bhukti* is that emotion directed toward the object of *bhakti*, namely, God Himself, who is of the nature of infinite love. Sri Ramakrishna said: "Be a *bhakta*, but don't be a *boka*!"[64] In Bengali, *boka* means a fool.

In the world there are too many fools passing as devoted to God for want of the strength of *jnana*, knowledge, and *buddhi*, reason. It is such devotees that are cheated by pretentious *gurus* and miracle-mongers. A true devotee cannot be cheated by anybody. But, unfortunately we find in all countries many devotees becoming easy prey to such imposters. Thus, they are predisposed to be cheated because they have dispensed with all knowledge and reason in their religious life. They are not interested in truth, but only in a little sentimentality or some religious sensationalism. When people understand religion correctly, that it is a science and, as science, we shall see an ever greater flowering of true religion as *dynamic spirituality* and the gradual withering away of the current noisy, showy, and static piety and piety-fringed worldliness so often mistaken by people as religion.

The great spiritual teachers of India were, like modern physical scientists, teachers of verified and verifiable truths. These are what we get from the *Upanishads*, the *Bhagavad Gita*, and from the books dealing with teachers like Buddha, Sri Ramakrishna, and Swami Vivekananda. In fact, one great utterance of the Buddha, which is worth repeating, is the exhortation to rationally examine a teaching before believing in it, which was included earlier as the Address to the Kalamas. On the subject of secrecy also, Buddha has said something that it would be advisable for all students to keep in mind, both students of science and students of religion, so that we shall have a total scientific revolution in the outer physical world as well as in the inner spiritual world. Addressing his disciple, Ananda, Buddha said: Secrecy does not belong to the *Tathagata* (Buddha). Buddha's teaching was open; it was *ehi passa, ehi passa,* come and see, come and see, as he himself described it. And he added: Secrecy belongs to three things, O Ananda. What are they? Secrecy belongs to priestly knowledge, to false doctrines, and to prostitutes![65]

These are Buddha's weighty words. If people will assimilate the spirit of these two utterances of the Buddha, we shall witness the flowering of true religion and true science everywhere.

The scientific temper and attitude, with its passion for truth and stress on verification of conclusions is thus common training for religion and for science, as understood in Vedanta. A scientist discovers some truth in the laboratory; it is published in a scientific journal. Another scientist checks it and verifies it. Still it is not enough. Several other research workers recheck it. And it finally emerges as an established scientific truth. That was the process in the world of religion for the *Upanishads* also. A sage discovered the divine core behind the human physical, neural, and psychical dimensions; and it was called "the Atman," the "divine Self." Another sage took up this challenging conclusion, rechecked it, and found it to be true. Then it passed the test of several sages as well. Finally, it emerged as the truth about humanity, as the truth of the science-of-human-possibilities, proclaiming the infinite dimension of what to the senses such as our eyes, appear as a finite, organically limited individual. This is not, therefore, a mere opinion or personal view. It is the deepest truth about humanity, about everyone, and anyone can rediscover it for himself or herself. It is knowledge based on existing fact or truth, *vastu-tantra-jnana*, as described by Shankaracharya in his *Brahma-Sutras* commentary.[66]

The message is: *vedahametam*, I have realized This. I have known This, not that I just believe in This! All and everyone can also realize This. Note the language when a verified and verifiable truth is being communicated. From these ancient sages like Prajapati, Gargi,[67] and Yajnavalkya, Varuna, Bhrgu, and Sanatkumara of the *Upanishads* over three thousand years ago to Sri Ramakrishna in our own time, this is the authentic temper and language of India's spirituality.

Human Being in Depth: Consciousness Itself

In thus presenting the universe in its fundamental aspect as Pure Consciousness only, Vedanta does not *destroy* the universe or its matter and separate intelligent beings, but only illumines the true nature of them all . . .

HUMAN BEING IN DEPTH: CONSCIOUSNESS ITSELF

The importance of the study of consciousness is being forced upon the modern world through the increasing recognition that the serious crises of our time can be resolved only through a change in consciousness and not through further technological changes in the outer physical world. As forcefully expressed by John White in the book, *The Highest State of Consciousness:* "Political action, social work, this *ism* that *ology*, are all incomplete, futile actions unless accompanied by a new and elevated mode of awareness. The ultimate action, then, is no action at all except to change consciousness. In other words, *the true revolution is revelation.*[1]

The study of mind and consciousness received recognition from physical science only recently when the American Association for the Advancement of Science accepted the Parapsychological Association, the international professional society for psychical research, as an affiliate organization on 30 December 1969. And John White predicts a healthy development in the field, in the coming years: "In the years ahead, explorations of the self will be integrated and therefore interdisciplinary. They will bring together physicists, psychical researchers, psychophysiologists, religious leaders, and workers from other professions.

"If the borders between self and environment can be made to disappear, this is likely to have profound effects in man's attitude to his environment, both social and physical. If the self is experienced as actually embracing other people, self-consciousness becomes social consciousness."[2]

Warning against the rigid attitude of certain psychiatrists, who blindly follow Freud's lead in defining all mystic perceptions of a fundamental spiritual unity in the universe as a regression to the primary cognition of the infantile or primitive state, Arthur J. Deikman, in his comments immediately preceding the report on *What Mysticism Is* by G.A.P. (Group for the Advancement of Psychiatry), says: "This naive reductionism is all the more striking in the context of the numerous reports from physicists indicating that the world is actually more like the one that the mystics describe than the one on which psychology and psycho-analysis are based. Contemporary scientists have ample evidence that the world of discrete objects is an illusion, a function of the particular scale of our perception and time sense. For them, it is commonplace that the phenomena of biology and physics point to a continuous world of gradients, not a collection of objects . . .

. . . "If our profession is to advance, we must recognise our defences against ideas that would change our assumptions. Mysticism, studied seriously, challenges basic tenets of Western cultures: a) the primacy of reason and intellect; b) the separate, individual nature of man; c) linear organisation of time. Great mystics, like our own great scientists, envision the world as being larger than those tenets, as transcending our traditional views. By not recognizing our defensiveness, and by permitting our vision to be narrowed so as to exclude the unfamiliar, we betray our integrity as psychiatrists, showing no more capacity for freedom from prejudice than persons totally ignorant of psycho-dynamics—perhaps less . . .

. . . "If we learn nothing more from mystics than the need for humility, they will have contributed greatly to Western culture in general and to the profession of psychiatry in particular."[3]

It is significant, that in this modern scientific age, the study of consciousness is receiving serious attention, not only from Western psychologists, but also from Western physicists and biologists. So we find Robert E. Ornstein, editor of *The Nature of Human Consciousness,* in the introduction to the book, quoting physicist Robert Oppenheimer's remark on how scientific and mystical ways of knowing are complementary to each other: "These two ways of thinking, the way of time and history, and the way of eternity and timelessness, are both part of man's effort to comprehend the world in which he lives. Neither is comprehended in the other nor reducible to it, . . . each supplementing the other, neither telling the whole story."[4]

Discussing the nature of knowledge and pointing out the limitations of the knowledge derived from physical science, Charles T. Tart says: "Blackburn [in the selection here preceding] noted that many of our most talented young people are 'turned off' to science. . . . I have seen the same rejection of science by many of the brightest students in California, and the problem is indeed serious. . . .

". . . Knowledge may be defined as an immediately given experimental feeling of congruence between two different kinds of experience, a matching. One set of experiences may be regarded as perceptions of the external world, of others, of oneself; the second set may be regarded as a theory, a scheme, a system of understanding. Reason is a tool, and a tool that is wielded in the service of assumptions, beliefs, and needs, which are not themselves subject to reason. The irrational, or, better yet, the arational, will not disappear from the human situation. Our immense success in the development of the physical sciences has not been particularly successful in formulating better philosophies of life, or increasing our real knowledge of ourselves. The sciences we have developed to date are not very human sciences. They tell us how to do things, but give us no scientific insights on questions of what to do, what not to do, or why to do things."[5]

The open-mindedness of these writers and thinkers is a healthy sign. The contemporary developments in modern psychotherapy include the investigation into consciousness; and this investigation is being highly influenced by Eastern systems of Yoga, Vedanta, Taoism, and Zen. These influences are enriching fundamentally its theory and technique. Many modern books are being published with the study of consciousness as the theme. These influences are converting modern psychology and psychotherapy from a merely curative to a preventive science.[6] When this preventive science develops, it will develop into the science of spirituality as happened in ancient India through developments in depth psychology. India developed psychology very early, by which she then developed religion into a science of spiritual experience.

This is the strength behind Vedanta, Buddhism, and Jainism; all of them are based on a depth psychology. In the West, neither theology nor psychology received the help of this depth study of the human psyche. But psychology in the West is developing into this depth dimension by contact with Eastern depth psychologies. Religion also is putting increasing stress on its experiential dimension.

THE FIELD CONCEPT IN VEDANTA AND MODERN SCIENCE

When we deal with the subject of consciousness, we deal with the subject of *experience*. Experience is a new datum that evolution exhibits with the appearance of the living cell, converting evolution from the cosmic to the organic dimension. The living cell discloses the attributes of *sat* and *cit*. The cell discloses the presence of consciousness in its rudimentary experience, or awareness, of its environment. From then on, evolution is a steady unfoldment of consciousness with every step in the development of the organism. This development achieves a breakthrough with the appearance of Homo sapiens on the evolutionary scene, when experience discloses a new dimension of awareness, namely, self-awareness, along with the non-self awareness, a subject awareness along with an object awareness. At this level, consciousness enlarges its bounds, resulting in our near-total understanding and dominance of the external environment and a slight knowledge of ourselves as the subject, the 'Self.' Cognition or knowledge rises, at this stage, from the primary to the secondary logical intellectual level.

All knowledge begins as a subject knowing an object. At the farthest reach of this process, through the entire gamut of acquiring positivistic knowledge, Vedanta discovered that the mystery of humanity and nature could be solved first, through an initial inner penetration to understanding the nature of the subject, the Self, the knower, while investigating the nature of the objective world, followed later, by a daring investigation into the nature of knowledge itself. Between the experienced, the experiencer, and the experience, Vedanta entered into the inquiry into the nature of experience itself. Vedanta discovered that experience or knowledge, meaning wisdom, as the Consciousness-Field, and all objects and all subjects as its passing configurations, and thus resolved the distinctions between knowledge, the knower, and the object of knowledge, which are known in Vedanta as *triputi*, the triple group. And it termed the ultimate Reality of Atman or Brahman as *Anubhava-svarupa*, or *jnana-swarupa* or *cit-svarupa*—"of the very nature of Experience," "of the very nature of Knowledge," "of the very nature of Consciousness."

Some of the greatest utterances of the *Upanishads* convey this "Truth of all Truths"—*Satyasya Satyam [Brhadaranyaka Upanishad* II.1.20]; *Prajnanam Brahma*—"Brahman is Pure Consciousness" [*Aitareya Upanishad* V.3]; *Satyam Jnanam Anantam Brahma*—"Brahman is Truth, Consciousness, and Infinity" [*Taittirya Upanishad* II.1]. *Sarvam hyetat Brahma, ayam atma Brahma, so'ayam atma catushpat*—"All this manifested universe is Brahman, this Self is Brahman, this Self manifests Itself through the four states (waking, dream, deep sleep and the *turiya* or the transcendental" [*Mandukya Upanishad* II.].

This development in ancient Vedanta has its parallel in modern physics, in the revolutionary concept of the electromagnetic *field* introduced by Michael Faraday (1791–1867) and James Clerk Maxwell (1831–1879) earlier, who replaced the mechanical concept of force, then prevailing, by the more subtle concept of the *force-field*, which has its own reality and could be investigated without reference to any material entities. This revolution was carried further in this century by the discoveries of the quantum and gravitational fields by nuclear science and relativity theory. This revolutionary field concept has now entered embryology in the biological sciences. According to biologist Richard Davenport, "The unit of organisation that embodies the attributes of positional information in individuating systems is the *embryonic field*. We will define an embryonic field as an embryonic system, or part of such a system, that contains constituent elements that only acquire their potential properties in relation to a common source of positional information, but also can re-establish the informational system, its constituent elements, and their responses, following the disturbance of spatial relationships within the system. . . .

" . . . From a consideration of the previous properties of fields, it is clear that they provide the constraints on cellular function that are necessary for differentiation and individuation. If there is any single key to an understanding of ontogeny, it is the embryo-logical field. When embryological systems are reduced to their essential components and properties, these are found to coincide with the properties of fields. Embryological systems cannot be reduced beyond their constituent fields without the disappearance of the very properties that characterize ontogeny. The egg is a field and can be subdivided only to the extent that preserves its field properties. During the later development, the original single field of the egg becomes subdivided into smaller and restricted fields, which have essentially the same basic properties operating on a small scale."[7]

Again, relating biology to the revolutionary developments in nuclear physics, Richard Davenport says: "Biology must profit from the experience of physics so that it can become consicous of what occurs during analysis and accept the fact that each level of organization is manifested by unique forces, since it contains unique interactions. Life is distinct from non-life, both in the fact that it is organized by forces that do not constrain inorganic systems, and in the constraint of its lower levels of structure by the weaker interactions of higher levels. By such a unique pattern of constraint, evolution has produced the organic world from which our description of physical reality has emerged through binding the observer and the observed in a system of interactions that are constrained by the forces of consciousness. Therefore, each level must be equally accepted as a legitimate description of a local experience of the universal forces of ordering that produce the aging of this world."[8]

Finally, pleading for the release of science as a whole from the mechanistic terms and concepts of just one of its departments, Richard Davenport concludes his book: "Biology may yet produce the next great scientific revolution. However, it will not do so by any imitation of mechanical physics, but only by a recognition of the legitimacy of its own structural domain, and of the constraint of this domain on the character of our knowledge. At the same time, it must accept that all levels of description are equally insufficient. In this ability to accept such a realization the greatest power of our descriptive actitivies lies—the power that enables us to see into our own nature. This insight will emerge from our failure to force experience to agree with our egoistic expectations, and will enable us to understand the true center of convergence that supports all structure and, thereby, to delight in all its levels of manifestation. This insight will not, as some assume, produce the end of science but will allow us to live in the full meaning of the term scientia, "to know." By relinquishing our partiality, we can create a neutral space in which, little by little, we will come to know that the reality our consciousness has fashioned is symbolic in the deepest sense and ceaselessly points toward that from which all experience flows – the ineffable one that is Nature!"[9]

Richard Davenport's observations on consciousness are, to say the least, not only thought-provoking, but also inspiring.

THE COMPREHENSIVE NATURE OF ATMAN-BRAHMAN AS CONSCIOUSNESS-FIELD

It is relevant in this context to point out the comprehensiveness of the Vedantic conception of Nature so as to include the physical, the biological, and the spiritual in the unity of Pure Consciousness, which is the meaning of God in Vedanta. Says Sri Krishna in the *Gita*, identifying Himself as the infinite Self of all [VII.4–6]:

> Earth, water, fire, air, space, mind, intellect and ego sense – this is my Nature (*prakrti*) divided eightfold.
>
> This is (My) lower (*prakrti*) but different from it, know thou, O mighty armed, My higher *prakrti* – the principle of intelligence, by which this universe is sustained.
>
> Know that these (two *prakrtis*) are the womb of all beings; I am the origin (maintenance and) dissolution of the whole universe.

Commenting on the last verse, Shankaracharya says: "Through this two-fold Nature, (lower) *prakrti* and (higher) *prakrti*, I, who am the omniscient God (being of the nature of infinite pure Consciousness), am the cause of this universe."[10]

There are several words in Sanskrit as equivalents of the English word, consciousness: *cit, prajna, jnapti, jnana, bodha, samvit*; according to contexts, they may mean infinite Pure Consciousness, knowledge, wisdom, and so forth.

The *Panchadashi* gives a lucid description of *samvit* as the eternal and non-dual Pure Consciousness, Brahman [I.7]:

> In all the countless months, years, ages, and aeons, which are past and which are yet to come, *Samvit*, which is one and self-luminous, does neither rise nor set.

The *Srimad Bhagavatam*, in a majestic utterance conveying a synoptic vision, describes the ultimate Reality as *advayam jnanam*, non-dual Pure Consciousness [I.2.11]:

> Knowers of Truth declare that the Truth of one and the same non-dual *jnanam*, Pure Consciousness, is spoken of as Brahman (by the *jnanis* or philosophers), as *para-matman*, the Supreme Self (by the yogis of mystics), and as *Bhagavan*, the All-loving God, (by the bhaktas or devotees).

Pure Consciousness is known as Brahman or Shiva, in its transcendental quiescent aspect, and as *Maya* or *Sakti*, in its immanent dynamic aspect; and both are one, like the unity of physical energy in its two aspects of being in contained and released states.

Shankaracharya presents "the goal of all Vedanta as the realization of the unity and infinitude of the Atman as Pure Consciousness," in his *Brahma-Sutra* Commentary [Sutra 4]. Nuclear physicist Erwin Schroedinger, as already quoted earlier, echoes this Vedantic truth that Consciousness is a singular of which the plural is unknown.

Modern subatomic physics is now in the position of the ancient Sankhya philosophy, in its reduction of the observed into the unity of the quantum field while retaining multiplicity in the dimension of the observer. The Sankhya achieved the unification of all non-self in its *pradhana* or *prakrti* or Nature, while retaining, however, self or subject. The unity of the Self and the unity of the Self and the non-self were achieved in Advaita, or non-dualistic philosophy, in its vision of Atman Brahman unity.

The great theme of Atman-Brahman is now being reflected in the writings of Erich Jantsch in his book, *Evolution and Consciousness*, where he writes:

> The Vedic concept of the correspondence between *atman*, the true essence of self (or reality within), and *brahman*, the true essence of reality without, is perhaps the most cogent expression of such an identity, though ultimately in terms of structure.

And later he says:

> Thus the process of searching and activating self-images of man is the real *re-ligio* . . . , the linking backward to our own origins in which *brahman* and *atman* become one.[11]

Modern physics has yet to achieve a complete and satisfactory unified theory comprehending electromagnetic and gravitational phenomena. Even if this unified field theory is firmly established in the future, the problem of unifying the *Prakrti* and *Purusha*, the observed and the observer, will haunt science's search for ultimate unity. Physicists like Fritjof Capra present the Brahman of the Vedanta as a more comprehensive background reality of the universe than modern physicist's Nature:

> The conception of physical things and phenomena as transient manifestations of an underlying fundamental entity is not only a basic element of quantum field theory, but also a basic element of the Eastern world view. Like Einstein, the Eastern mystics consider this underlying entity as the only reality: all its phenomenal manifestations are seen as transitory and illusory. This reality of the Eastern mystic cannot be identified with the quantum field of the physicist, because it is seen as the essence of *all* phenomena in this world and, consequently, is beyond all concepts and ideas. The quantum field, on the other hand, is a well defined concept which only accounts for some of the physical phenomena. Nevertheless, the intuition behind the physicist's interpretation of the subatomic world in terms of the quantum field is closely paralleled by that of the Eastern mystic who interprets his or her experience of the world in terms of an ultimate underlying reality. Subsequent to the emergence of the field concept, physicists have attempted to unify the various fields into a single fundamental field, which would incorporate all physical phenomena. Einstein, in particular, spent the last years of his life searching for such a unified field. The Brahman of the Hindus, like the Dharmakaya of the Buddhists and the Tao of the Taoists, can be seen, perhaps, as the ultimate unified field from which spring not only the phenomena studied in physics, but all other phenomena as well.[12]

The material universe of daily experience, which physical science has set about to study, will reveal its true form, as condensations of Pure Consciousness, as *isavasyam idam sarvam yat kinca jagatyam jagat*: All this manifested changing universe is enveloped by God, as the *Isha Upanishad* proclaims in its opening verse, when physics and all physical science dissociates the "matter" it studies from the dogma of materialism.

Gaudapada, the preceptor of Shankaracharya, in his *Mandukyakarika*, proclaims that the non-causal Pure Consciousness is realized by the non-causal pure knowledge, and salutes the teacher who discovered and taught this philosophic and spiritual vision of Advaita, non-duality, in two famous verses [III.33, IV.1]:

> Beyond all conceptual thinking is *jnanam*, spiritual knowledge, and is ever non-different from the knowable Reality: Brahman, the sole knowable Reality, is unborn (beyond Causality) and eternal: the non-causal knowledge realizes the non-causal (Brahman).
>
> I salute that best among the bi-peds (persons), who has realized, through knowledge which is infinite like space, the non-separateness of all ob-

jects, which are also infinite like space, with the object of the knowledge search (Brahman).

Millennia before the views of John Welwood, John White, Robert E. Ornstein and others quoted earlier, the ancient Indian lawgiver Manu said that all higher spiritual truths are obtained only through inner penetration and the raising of consciousness to higher and higher levels *Manu Samhita* [VI.82]:

All these that have been expounded earlier (about the realization of the non-dual Pure Consciousness), are the products of meditation; none bereft of the knowledge of the Atman can, verily, enjoy the fruits of their labor (in peace and joy).

THE CHARIOT AS IMAGERY IN HUMANITY'S SPIRITUAL JOURNEY

Speaking on preparations for the higher life, Swami Vivekananda said:

Meditation is the one thing. Meditate! The greatest thing is meditation. It is the nearest approach to spiritual life – the mind meditating. It is the one moment in our daily life that we are not at all material – the Soul thinking of itself, free from all matter – this marvelous touch of the Soul![13]

The *Upanishads* view the human personality, consisting of the body, the sense organs, mind, intellect, and the soul, in the light of the mighty evolutionary movements of nature. The *Katha Upanishad* employs a beautiful imagery – the imagery of the chariot to illustrate the evolutionary advance at the human level:

Know the Atman as the master within the chariot, and the body, verily as the chariot; know the *buddhi*, enlightened reason, as the charioteer, and the *manas* (incipient mind), verily as the reins.

The sense-organs, they say, are the horses, and the roads for them to travel are the sense objects. The wise call Him (namely, the Atman) the enjoyer or the experiencer (when He is united with the body, senses and mind).

That one who is devoid of right understanding and with *manas* mind always undisciplined, the senses become uncontrolled, like the uncontrolled horses of the charioteer.

That one who is possessed of right understanding and with mind always disciplined, the senses become controlled, like the controlled horses of a charioteer.

And that one who is devoid of right understanding, with *manas* (mind) not disciplined and always impure, never attains that goal, but gets into the repetitive experience of worldliness.

> But that one who is possessed of right understanding, with *manas* (mind) disciplined and ever pure, reaches that goal whence there is no return to worldliness again.
>
> That one who has *vijnana*, or enlightened reason, for the charioteer, and a (disciplined) *manas* (mind) as the reins – that one verily attains the end of the journey in that supreme divine state of Universality.[14]

This imagery tells us that an individual has an inner journey to perform in the context of the outer journey in the world of space and time. The world of sight and sound, of touch, taste, and smell, is the environment for both the outer journey and the inner one. The inner journey is a spiritual journey of inward penetration, by training the psychophysical energies and raising the mind and consciousness to higher and higher levels. As the chariot gets its energy of movement from the horses, the body gets its energy of movement from the sense organs, consisting of the nervous system and the brain. The organs of perception and the organs of action convert the animal body into a center of the most dynamic activity in nature. But at the level of the senses themselves, this activity is mostly uncoordinated and, therefore, not fit for purposes beyond mere organic satisfactions and survival. It is this coordination that is provided by *manas*, or incipient mentality, which Swami Vivekananda renders as "mind indecisive." It is even treated as merely a sixth sense organ. As in the case of the horses, the reins, meant to control them, involve a charioteer to hold the reins. In the human system, this is the function of *buddhi* or enlightened reason. And behind it there is the driver of the chariot, whose journey it is. The remaining items comprise the equipment for the journey.

Mere external journey in the world of space and time is what is termed *samsara* or worldliness, which means stagnation at the organic and psychological levels. The *Upanishad* considers this as the spiritual death of the person, which is more serious than physical death in the case of a species so high in evolution. Life's journey, whether outward or inward, in order to be successful, needs the contributions of all the constituents of the human personality: the body, the sense organs, the mind and the reasoning faculty. This cannot happen unless the mind and the reasoning faculty are trained and disciplined into their true forms. The true form of the mind is its pure state, when it is aligned with the reasoning faculty. Then alone it can stand the stress and strain involved in its unique situation as being between the powerful and initially opposite forces of the sensate thoughts and the enlightened reason. All psychic breakdown is the snapping of the mind. The true form of the reasoning faculty is its pure state as enlightened reason, when it is independent of the mind and the sense organs and functions as their guide and master. This is the source of far-sight and foresight. It then reflects the pure Light of Consciousness of the Atman behind it.

When free from the inebriations arising from the indigestion of wealth, power, sexuality, knowledge, pedigree, drugs, and wine, the reasoning faculty becomes luminous and calm, steady and sure. This kind of reason is the best guide in life's journey. It denotes the fusion of intelligence, imagination, and will in their purest forms. Its impact on life is irresistible as well as wholesome. The *Gita*, therefore, says that the Atman is realized by the enlightened reason (*buddhi*) and is unattainable by the sense organs or the sensate-bound mind (*manas*) – *buddhi grahyam atindriyam*.[15]

When the individual's psychophysical energy is directed by enlightened intelligence, something wonderful happens. Every step of life's journey is accompanied by a steady rise in the quality of life energy.

This enlightened intelligence, the *buddhi*, then becomes free from thraldom to the sense organs and from the service of mere organic survival. This freeing of *buddhi*, through the freeing of its physical instrument, the cerebral system, was achieved by nature in human beings through evolutionary processes initiated even in the prehuman stage. This achievement was referred to as homeostasis by Grey Walter, who in describing it maintained that ". . . With this arrangement, other parts of the brain are left free for functions not immediately related to the vital engine or the senses, for functions surpassing the wonders of homeostasis itself."[16] We are a unique specimen of evolution, holding the key to the mystery of nature, to the purpose of life, and to the meaning of all existence.

Our psychophysical system is a miniature universe in itself. The immensity of its interior dimension is obscured by the smallness of its external physical covering or *kosa* (sheath), as Vedanta terms it. In his thought-provoking book, *The Self-Organizing Universe*, Erich Jantsch has stated: "We contain the entire evolution within us, but it is orchestrated to a fuller and richer extent than in less complex life forms."[17]

The body and the surrounding world constitute the gross outer fringes of reality. This is reality as revealed by the sense organs. As we penetrate into the interior, we come across subtler and more immense aspects of reality; these are revealed only by the mind. With the advance of knowledge, the conviction is borne in upon us that, if ever there is an eternal, changeless, and, accordingly, infinite dimension to reality, it must lie in the center of consciousness. The discovery of such a center depends upon a mighty searching penetration, and in the process, it also will reveal the nature of the various layers or sheaths covering the inner reality. This is what the Indian sages – Satyakama, Sanatkumara, Narada, Varuna, and many others – did, including the great Buddha of a later age. This is what the *Upaṇishads* convey to us in words that bear the stamp of authentic experience.

THE SPIRITUAL JOURNEY AS INNER PENETRATION

In the course of this inner penetration to the Atman, we come across, says Vedanta, not only subtler dimensions of reality, but also more immense resources of energy. The first form of energy that becomes manifest in a human being, even in the fetus, is his or her muscular energy. The muscle power is the outermost and grossest dimension of human energy. This muscle power of a human being, or of a horse, is insignificant compared to the multimillion horsepower rockets of modern space technology.

However, behind the muscle, there is a tiny nerve fiber. It is subtle compared to the large muscle, but cut out that nerve fiber and the muscle is dead. Thus, at the very outset of our investigation, we realize that behind the gross muscle power there is a subtle, but more significant and more immense energy system in the nerves. Investigating further, we find that, behind the nervous system, there is a more subtle psychic energy system, sustaining and controlling that nervous system. If that psychic system breaks down, the muscle and the nerve will become powerless to function. Thus we see that, as we go deeper into ourselves, we come across subtler energies within. Further, we also note that, as we progress from the gross to the subtle, human energy resources become more and more immense in quantity, quality, and range. The ancient sages of the *Upanishads* successfully tried to penetrate into the depths of humanity with their highly trained and pure minds.

Penetrating behind the psychic system, they discovered the infinite and most subtle, the most immense spiritual energy system in the Atman, the true Self of each one of us. It is this discovery that is conveyed by that short *mantra* from the *Chandogya Upanishad: Tat tvam asi* – "That thou art."[18]

Through this investigation and experience, Vedanta discovered the profound truth about human nature, just as modern physics discovered the truth of the immense energies hidden at the nuclear core of a lump of matter, that human energy resources are organized on an ascending scale of subtlety, immensity, and inwardness: (*suksma, mahantasca, pratyagatmabhutasca*), in the language of Shankaracharya, giving the meaning of the term *para*, higher, used in the verses to be presently quoted in the *Katha Upanishad* [III.10.11]. This subtlety, immensity, and inwardness reach their final consummation in the Atman, the pure and non-dual Consciousness.

The energy output of a machine will be exactly the same as the energy input, be it gas, diesel, electric, or nuclear power. But the energy output in a human being, while generally following this law, will often be different. We cannot say that human energy output is exactly equivalent to his or her food or intellectual consumption. Many people consume much food with very little energy output, while some men and women exhibit much energy in life and work while eating very little food. Vedanta speaks of three types of energy present in us: *bahu balam* or muscular energy, *buddhi balam* or intellectual energy, and *Atma balam* or *yoga balam* or spiritual energy. It is the release of that third type of energy that makes for high moral character and acts as a preventive in regard to psychic and social distortions and breakdowns.

Buddha, Jesus, Sri Ramakrishna, and similar spiritual personalities manifest a type of world-moving energy, during their lifetime and also long after their physical death, which is out of all proportion to their food or intellectual consumption. A science of our total nature has to take note of this truth that, with respect to each of us, the energy resource has to be defined as food plus the consciousness level at which he or she lives and works as well as the philosophy of each.

Speaking on "Vedanta in All Its" Phases at Calcutta in 1897, Swami Vivekananda presented India's experience of humanity's search for truth gracefully rising, from the field of external physical nature, to the strange new field of the internal nature of humanity, to the "within" aspect of nature:

> Just as the Greek mind, or the modern European mind, wants to find the solution of life, and of all the sacred problems of being, by searching into the external world, so also did our forefathers; and just as the Europeans failed, they failed also. But the Western people never made a move more; they remained there; they failed in the search for the solutions of the great problems of life and death in the external world; and there they remained, stranded. Our forefathers also found it impossible, but were bolder in declaring the utter helplessness of the senses to find the solution. Nowhere else was the answer put than in the Upanishads – [*Taittirya Upanishad* II.4]: *yato vaco nivattanta aprapya manasa saha* – "From whence words come back reflected, along with the mind, without attaining 'The Truth'"; *na tatra caksuh gacchati, na vak gacchati* – "There the eye cannot go, nor can speech reach." [*Kena Upanishad* I.3].
>
> There are various sentences which declare the utter helplessness of the senses; but they did not stop there. They fell back upon the internal nature of man; they went to get the answer from their own soul. They became introspective. They gave up external nature as a failure, as nothing could be done there, as no hope, no answer, could be found. They discovered

> that dull, dead matter would not give them truth; and they fell back upon the shining soul of man, and there, the answer was found.[19]

Referring to the advance attained by ancient India in this science of human possibilities, Max Muller observed:

> But if it seems strange to you that the old Indian philosophers should have known more about the soul than the Greek or medieval or modern philosophers, let us remember that, however much the telescopes for observing the stars of heaven have been improved, the observatories of the soul have remained much the same.[20]

The *Katha Upanishad* gives us a glimpse into this inner penetration in verses ten and eleven of its third chapter. Introducing these verses, Shankaracharya says in his commentary: "Now that state, which is to be attained (through the spiritual journey), a journey which begins with the sense organs which are gross, and proceeds through comparatively subtler and subtler aspects – that state is to be realized as the *pratyagatman*, the Inner Self."[21] In order to convey this truth, the *Upanishad* proceeds as follows:

> The sense-objects (in their nuclear dimensions) are *para* that is, higher, than the sense-organs, the mind (*manas*) is higher than the sense objects; enlightened reason (*buddhi*) is higher than the mind (*manas*); the *mahan atma* (great self that is, the Cosmic Mind) is higher than *buddhi*.
>
> The *avyakta* (undifferentiated Nature) is higher than the *mahat* (Cosmic Mind); the Purusha (the infinite Self) is higher than the *avyakta*. There is nothing higher than the Purusha; that *is* the finale, that *is* the supreme goal.[22]

The layers spoken of in these verses as covering reality are described as *kosas* or sheaths in the *Taittiriya Upanishad* [second and third books (II.2–5. and III.10]. They are five in number: *annamaya*, material or physical, comprising the body and the encompassing physical nature revealed by the sense organs; *pranamaya*, *manomaya*, and *vijnanamaya*, corresponding to the three layers of the sense organs, *manas*, and *buddhi*; and *anandamaya*, corresponding to the *avyakta* or undifferentiated nature. *Indriyas, manas* and *buddhi* may stand for the biospherical, the psychical, and the noospherical of modern enumeration.

Studying the whole human phenomenon and seeking for the true focus of the experience of selfhood at the core of the personality, Vedanta discovered these five sheaths, also known as the three bodies, namely, the gross body, the subtle, and the causal bodies, in all of which, as remarked by Dr. S. Radhakrishnan in his translation of the *Gita*: "There is no changeless center or immortal nucleus in these pretenders to selfhood."[23]

The body, the sense organs, the mind, and the ego, all lay claim to being the Self. Before inquiry, a person takes one or other of them as his or her self. But philosophical inquiry reveals their not-self character. It reveals each one of them as an object with the reflected light of consciousness, and not as a subject that is self-luminous. Each is a *samghata* or aggregate, in the terminology of Vedanta and Buddha, and as such, subject to change and destruction.

The search for the Self must leave them behind and proceed deeper. If nothing is discovered beyond these changing not-self elements, one is right in resigning oneself to nihilism in philosophy and pragmatism in life. Vedanta, however, finds in the facts of experience enough intimations of a changeless reality, which justify a more penetrating investigation of experience by reason. This scrutiny of experience revealed to Vedanta the presence of a changeless subject or knower at the center of the knowing or observing process, at the core of the human personality.

As affirmed by Shankaracharya: "There *is* some entity, eternal by nature, the basis of the experience of ego-sense, the witness of the three states (of waking, dream, and deep sleep), and distinct from the five sheaths. Who knows everything that happens in the waking, dream, and deep sleep states; who is aware of the presence or absence of mind and its functions, and who is the basis of the ego-sense."[24]

The discovery of the truth of the immortal Self behind the mortal body-mind complex is the universal gospel, or good news, which the *Upanishads* have left as their immortal legacy to all humanity. It was not just an intellectual discovery through a speculative venture. It was a spiritual realization containing vast possibilities for the intellectual and moral life of humanity. It underwrites and guarantees the *precious value of freedom of the human spirit*. Being a spiritual discovery, it is proclaimed to the world at large not as an intellectual formula to be believed in, but a spiritual fact to be realized by every human being. The discovery by a few is to be translated into a re-discovery by the many. For it is the birthright of one and all. This makes it a compelling message for everyone.

The *Katha Upanishad* testifies to the universal appeal of this message. In verse twelve of its third chapter, the *Upanishad* spells out the universality of the Atman, and its verifiability in life [III.12]:

> This Atman (being) hidden in all beings, is not manifest (to all). But (It) can be realised by all who are trained to inquire into subtle truths by means of their sharp and subtle reason.

As the eternal subject or knower, it is an ever present datum of experience and not a mere logical construction; but it does not reveal itself as such to one and all. Not to speak of ordinary people, even great scholars fail to comprehend the Atman. The verse gives the reason – "It is subtle, hidden." It is a mysterious presence. It is a splendor, but imprisoned, in the language of Robert Browning in his poem *Paracelsus*. Therefore – "It is not manifest"; – "since (it is) unknown to one whose reason is not refined or purified,"[25] comments Shankaracharya. It is not present on the surface of experience. It is hidden in its depth.

Though a mystery, the Atman shall not always remain so. Though an unknown, Vedanta does not treat it as an unknowable. *Drsyate* – "It can be seen, realized," through pure enlightened reason, since it is an ever present datum of experience. What is the quality of the enlightened reason which achieves this? *Agryaya buddhya suksmaya* – "by enlightened reason which is sharp and subtle." Explaining the meaning of this, Shankaracharya says in his commentary:

> They are *suksmadarsinah* – "subtle seers" – who are trained, through seeing subtler and subtler realities as mentioned in the passage: "the objects are higher than the sense-organs", etc. (verses ten and eleven), to see the supremely subtle reality (of the *Purusha* or the Atman).[26]

The *Katha Upanishad* then proceeds, in verses thirteen and fifteen, to expound this extraordinary Vedantic discipline of inner penetration for the realization of the Atman and the sweet result of that penetration:

> Let the *prajna* (wise one) merge the speech in the mind (*manas*) and the mind in the *buddhi* (enlightened reason); let the wise one merge the *buddhi* in the Cosmic Mind, and merge that Cosmic Mind again in the Atman, which is all Peace.[27]

The Atman is significantly characterized as consisting of *shanti* (peace). Commenting on this Shankaracharya says:

> In the peace of the primary Atman (Real Self which is) characterized by the complete cessation of all differentiation, changeless, the innermost reality of all, and the witness of all the pulsations of *buddhi*.
>
> By realizing that Atman which is beyond sound, beyond taste, beyond smell, even beyond the *mahat* (Cosmic Mind), formless, imperishable, eternal, beginningless and endless, and immutable, (one) is liberated from the jaws of death.[28]

ARISE! AWAKE! AND STOP NOT UNTIL THE GOAL IS REACHED

In our external life, our consciousness handles external objects, but in our inner life, it is consciousness handling consciousness itself. Vedanta proclaims that something wonderful happens when we succeed in stilling the sense organs and the mind. It brings us face-to-face with the mystery of our own true self. Vedanta and yoga describe evolution at the human stage as this inner penetration to discover the infinite behind the finite, the immortal behind the mortal. Our mind is to be trained to penetrate into its own inner dimensions.

The technique of this inner penetration is meditation, supported by moral strength, which is achieved in the course of our journey in space and time in the context of human interactions in society. It is the scientifically trained mind that penetrates into the heart of the material world and discovers the truths, and disciplines the energies, hidden there. The same discipline of the mind, carried to higher and more subtle dimensions, helps us to penetrate into the heart of consciousness itself. In the science of the inner life, which Vedanta developed, and which can be termed "a science of human possibilities," to use Sir Julian Huxley's famous phrase, we have a study of humanity under various conditions of inner discipline, which has yielded results more wonderful and significant than those in the physical sciences. The human mind develops high subtlety and penetration power by spiritual training. The highest result of such disciplines of the energies of the inner life is total illumination—*jnana*, or *bodhi*, the state of spiritual incandescence, and creative peace.

When Buddha attained illumination on that blessed full moon night over twenty-five hundred years ago, he exclaimed in joy: the immortal has been gained by me; all bondage has been broken; I have attained what ought to be attained by a human being.[29]

The Vedanta therefore recognizes two levels of spirituality, namely, the spirituality of the secular ethical dimension, referred to as *dharma*, and the spirituality of the mystical dimension, referred to as *amrta*, in the *Upanishads* and the *Gita*. At the stage of *dharma*, a person starts on the spiritual journey of psychosocial evolution, in the language of modern biology, evolves from individuality to personality, and achieves ethical awareness, human concern, and happy interhuman relations. Thus, after fulfilling life in the social context, one continues the spiritual journey in the *amrta*, or the mystical or higher spiritual dimension, at every step of which his or her consciousness overcomes limitations, genetic as well as psychic, and expands and becomes universal. We become truly individuals only when we become universal, and this universality is our true nature, which becomes apparently dimmed and contracted by our genetic and psychic limitations, as well as by limitations arising from caste, creed, race, nationality, and sex awareness.

The raising of consciousness to higher spiritual levels begins even when we are in search of organic satisfactions. This raising is done by what the *Katha Upanishad* refers to, in the opening verses of its second chapter, in which the boy, Naciteka, is presented a choice between the pleasant and the good, by a discriminating positive attitude, wherein self-interest is put aside, and the good of all becomes prominent.

The ancient *Upanishads* and Buddha classify all developments of consciousness levels into two categories, namely, the *loka* and the *lokottara*. These are technical terms in Sanskrit with precise meanings in the science of human development. *Loka* means the sensory world. In the early stages of human development, consciousness functions at the sensory level (*loka*), and human development is achieved in the context of interaction with the outer natural and social environments, resulting in a slight inward growth to our true self and manifesting outwardly a more humanized interaction in the social context. After getting well established in this social context at the *loka* level with its rewards of ethical and moral awareness and sensibilities, consciousness gets the capacity and the urge to rise to the *lokottara* level, if it is not made stagnant and uncreative by inadequate philosophies of life at the sensory level.

Lokottara means trans-sensory. The word transcendental will be its near English equivalent. The capacity to rise to the *lokottara* level comes from the fulfillment of ethical demands. That is the meaning when the great world religions say that ethics and morality are the basis for all higher spiritual development into *samadhi* and *prajna*, meditation and wisdom or enlightenment in the words of Vedantic and Buddhistic teachings.

Over four thousand years ago, the sages of the *Upanishads* conveyed their transcendental experiences in inspired utterances full of rational conviction. These were taken up by other spiritual seekers who confirmed them. Some centuries later appeared the *Bhagavad Gita* with its message of a higher spiritual development in the very context of his or her life and action and interhuman relations. Some centuries later in the sixth century B.C. appeared Buddha who achieved enlightenment, or *bodhi*, on a blessed full moon night as a result of a courageous inward meditation and penetration. The nature of that courageous effort finds expression in his mighty resolve, which has been put into verse by a later writer in his book, *Lalitavistara* [XIa.57]:

> Let my body wither away on this seat,
> Let skin, bone, and flesh get dissolved;
> Without achieving enlightenment, difficult
> to achieve in many aeons,
> Never shall this body move away from this seat!

These transcendental or *lokottara* experiences raise consciousness beyond the limitations of the body, the sense organs, and the sense-bound mind and in addition beyond the network of time, space, and causality. Mortality pertains to the level of time, and immortality is the dimension beyond time. Similarly, conditioned by space, consciousness remains limited and splintered into separate bits. Transcendance of space is also transcendance of all splintering and multiplicity. Within causality, consciousness is bound by the cause and effect determinism; and above causality, it achieves its inherent freedom and spontaneity. In the highest spiritual realizations, consciousness realizes its own true nature as immortal, non-dual, and free. When one of the sages of the *Upanishads* realized within himself this highest truth about humanity, his joy, as was the case with Buddha later, could not be contained within himself, but burst out with good news for everyone everywhere, *Taittiriya Upanishad* [I.X.1]: "I am the immortal one. I am an effulgent and shining treasure, wise, immortal, undecaying and inexhaustible."

So spoke Trishanku after attaining the knowledge of the unity of the Self. Having realized his consciousness as immortal and non-dual, he shared with all humanity this knowledge of their common ground.

In the process of raising consciousness to higher levels, we come across one important truth, namely, the constant experience of a drag downward and the need for more energy to achieve the lift. Vedanta calls this drag by the term *"vasana"* or *"samskara,"* subtle innate impressions of past thoughts, actions, and attachments. The gravitational pulls of the non-spiritual parts of our being make this path out of bounds for any but the most heroic of persons – the *"dhiras"* – as the *Upanishads* term them. We have to reduce the downward pulls. This is the meaning of *renunciation* in its purest sense – a joyous and spontaneous giving up of something less valuable with a view to attaining something more valuable: the child giving up its toys in preference to books. To those who understand its value, renunciation of attachments and organic cravings becomes a spontaneous and joyous experience, like the leaving behind of excess baggage for an astronaut. There is no feeling of any sacrifice.

Most people need much practical help and guidance and several easy steps in this path, which is provided by Vedanta in its *bhakti* (devotional aspect), and in other paths of its practical science of spirituality. In these there is a legitimate place for rituals and other outward spiritual practices if the goal of spiritual growth is constantly kept in view. The *Katha Upanishad* summons all humanity to undertake this great adventure of raising consciousness to its highest level of purity, luminosity, and universality [III.14]:

> Arise! Awake! enlighten yourself by resorting to the great (teachers); like the sharp edge of a razor is that path, so say the sages, difficult to tread and hard to cross.

Overcoming the drag of the gravitational pulls of the organic system, and raising consciousness to higher levels, is a slow and steady process. It is to be treated as a converging life endeavor. It cannot be done by magic and tricks or by psychedelic drugs. Some people try to achieve it by high emotional excitements. But it does not help. Consciousness comes down when the excitement is abated and falls even further.

When you start controlling the senses and the mind and experience meditation and receive the touch of the divine within, a wonderful personality change occurs. One is lifted from creatureliness to freedom, from wretchedness to blessedness. What happens when we repeat the name of God with devotion in our hearts? This is described in *The Srimad Bhagavatam* [I.2.17]. Says the first verse:

> When the blessed divine Krishna, who lives in the hearts of all, hears the recitation of His name by the devotee, He gently wipes away all that is evil in the heart of the devotee; for He is the friend of (all) good people.

As the Hindus recite various names of God like Krishna, Shiva, Hari, and so forth, so in Roman Catholic Christianity we have the *mantras* like Ave Maria, so also other divine names in other religions. The next verse says:

> When most of the impurities of the heart have been removed by the practice of constant devotion to God, one's *bhakti*, or devotion to God, the most excellent and Holy One, becomes steady (while it was unsteady before).

Mind is devoted to God at some time; it loses all interest in spiritual life at another time. This is the condition when one begins the spiritual life. But, at this stage, the devotion becomes steady, like the compass needle constantly pointing to the north. Sorrows and failures cannot affect that steady devotion to God. In many Christian saints, we can study this kind of progress and development of steady devotion. That steadiness is the product of the mind when it is pure. What happens then? The next verse [I.2.19] explains it:

> In that state (of steady devotion), the mind (of the devotee) becomes freed from the pressures of passion, and inertia (forces of nature), and, unsmitten by (their bitter fruits of) lust and greed and other passions, it becomes steady in the peace of *sattva*, i.e., purity and calmness.

Impelled by the forces of *rajas* (passion) and inertia (*tamas*), the mind becomes inclined to evil, to come under the influence of the six enemies of humanity: lust, anger, greed, delusion, arrogance, and violence. Free from these forces, the mind shines pure in (*sattva*); it is the mind that is pure that can realize spirituality. "Blessed are the pure in heart, for they shall see God," says Jesus. And so the next verse [I.2.20] says:

> When the mind becomes tranquil (in *sattva*) through the practice of devotion to God, the devotee, who is now free from all sensory attachments, experiences the truth of God.

And, finally, what happens to the seeker through such realization? The last verse [I.2.21] answers:

> When the Divine Lord is realized within oneself, all the knots of the heart are broken, all doubts get destroyed, and all (ego-centered) actions and their *samskaras* (impressions) become eliminated.

These knots of the heart, what modern psychology calls "complexes," become broken. Too many complexes distort the human psyche; and complexes are formed when we do not have the spiritual strength to digest all experiences. Realization of the Blessed Lord, the One Self in all, in oneself, destroys all these knots completely. All the *samskaras* (impressions) that keep us chained to the sensory and genetic dimensions of life become burned up and eliminated in the fire of spiritual experience.

The technique of awakening the *kundalini*, our dormant psychic energies, as taught in some forms of yoga, are also a means for raising consciousness to higher levels. Vedanta and Sri Ramakrishna maintain that that awakening can be achieved as a by-product of a person's spiritual life through the paths of *bhakti*, *jnana*, and *karma* yogas. When, through these yogas, the seeker achieves spiritual awareness, it signifies also the awakening of the *kundalini*. That is why in the great spiritual books like the *Bhagavad Gita*, or in the teachings of Buddha, there is emphasis on moral and spiritual growth, but not on the *kundalini* awakening process, which is only like a barometer registering atmospheric pressure. To raise that pressure, you need not do anything within the barometer. You only lift it to higher altitudes and the raising of the atmospheric pressure follows as its by-product. Similarly, wherever moral and spiritual development are present, you can conclude that the *kundalini* has risen through the lower three centers and reached the fourth and higher centers. These paths, therefore, say: live the spiritual life and the *kundalini* awakening will follow as a matter of course.

Says Swami Saradananda, one of the direct disciples of Sri Ramakrishna and also his biographer [*Sri Ramakrishna the Great Master*, vol. 1, pp. 417–18]:

> Ah, how very simple were the words with which the Master explained to us these intricate facts of yoga! "You see," said he, "something goes

up creeping from the feet to the head. Consciousness continues to exist as long as this power does not reach the head; but as soon as it reaches the head, all consciousness is completely lost. There is no seeing or hearing anymore, much less of speaking. Who can speak? The very idea of *I* and *you* vanishes. While it goes up, I feel a desire to tell you everything—how many visions I experience, of what nature they are, etc. Until it comes to this place (showing the heart) or at most this place (showing the throat), speaking is possible, and I do speak; but the moment it goes up beyond this place (showing the throat), someone forcibly presses the mouth, as it were, and I lose consciousness."[30]

Again, in speaking about the *kundalini,* he said:

God is both within and without. From within He creates the various states of the mind. After passing through the six centers, the *jiva* (individual) goes beyond the realm of *maya* and becomes united with the Supreme Soul. This is the vision of God.[31]

The *Katha Upanishad* introduces this rising of consciousness to the transcendental (*amrta*) level, above the *dharma* level, as yoga, in Chapter and verses [VI. 9–11]:

His form is not within the field of sight; none can see Him with the eye; He is revealed in the (cavity of) the heart by the mind (*manas*) that is fully under the control of enlightened reason (*buddhi*). Those who realize this become immortal.

When the five sense organs of knowledge remain steady along with the mind (*manas*), and even enlightened reason (*buddhi*) does not flicker—that is the supreme state, say the sages.

They (the sages) consider that as yoga—the steady control of the sense organs; the yogi must then be vigilant; for yoga can be acquired and lost.

We get a beautiful description of the state of meditation, where the infinite Pure Consciousness shines in all His glory, from these six verses of remarkable clarity and perception in the *Gita* [VI.18–23:

When the completely disciplined mind rests in the Atman alone, free from longing after all desires, then is one called steadfast in yoga.

As a lamp sheltered from wind does not flicker, even so is the simile used for a yogi of disciplined mind practising concentration in the Atman.

When the mind, fully restrained by the practice of yoga, attains quietude, and when seeing the Self by the self, one is satisfied in the Self;

When he realizes that infinite bliss which is grasped by the (pure) *buddhi,* and which is beyond (the reach of) the sense-organs, and established wherein he never wavers from the truth (of the Self);

> And having obtained which, (he) regards no other gain superior to that, and wherein established, he is not shaken even by very heavy sorrow;
>
> Let that be known as the state called yoga – a state of disunion from (all) union with sorrow. This yoga should be practiced with determination, undisturbed by depression of heart.

Vedanta and yoga present the realization of the infinite Pure Consciousness as every individual's birthright, that its attainment raises a man or woman above all terrestrial and celestial beings, that it is to be had in this very world, in this very life, not in a postmortem heaven, and that many have attained this highest spiritual realization.

In the *Gita*, the indwelling God, in His incarnation as Krishna, proclaims this truth [IV.10]:

> Freed from attachment, fear and anger, absorbed in Me, taking refuge in Me (and) purified by the fire of asceticism of knowledge, many have attained to My Being.

The same is affirmed by Gaudapada in his *Mandukyakarika* in almost identical language [II.35]:

> Verily, this *nirvikalpa* (unconditioned *samadhi*) state, in which relative existence is ended and which is non-dual, *has been* realised by the wise, who are free from attachment, fear and anger, and who have gone beyond the (letter) of the Vedas (scriptures, through experiment and experience).

Having gone through these spiritual practices by way of the different yogas, the question may arise as it does in the second chapter of the *Gita*: "In what manner does an illumined soul speak? How does he (or she) sit? How does he (or she) walk?" Krishna replies:

He knows bliss in the Atman
And wants nothing else.
Cravings torment the heart:
He renounces cravings.
I call him illumined.

Not shaken by adversity,
Not hankering after happiness:
Free from fear, free from anger,
Free from the things of desire.
I call him a seer, and illumined.

The bonds of his flesh are broken.
He is lucky, and does not rejoice:
He is unlucky, and does not weep.
I call him illumined.

The tortoise can draw in its legs:
The seer can draw in his senses.
I call him illumined.

And the last two verses:

Water flows continually into the ocean
But the ocean is never disturbed:
Desire flows into the mind of the seer
But he is never disturbed.
The seer knows peace:
The man who stirs up his own lusts
Can never know peace.
He knows peace who has forgotten desire.
He lives without craving:
Free from ego, free from pride.
This is the state of enlightenment in Brahman:
A man does not fall back from it
Into delusion.
Even at the moment of death
He is alive in that enlightenment:
Brahman and he are one.[32]

ATMAN-BRAHMAN AS THE UNIFIED EXPERIENCE-FIELD

This is the reality that reveals itself to the discerning mind as the unchanging *sakshi* or witness of all the changing subjects and objects of the various states. Since it is not limited by any one particular state as the ego is, it is infinite. After the realization of this truth, one does not desire to protect or defend oneself, because of the realization of non-duality and the attainment of the state of fearlessness. All ideas of hatred, offense, self-protection, self-defense, and hiding, proceed from fear, from a feeling of inadequacy with respect to the environment. Realization of the Atman means realization of one's infinite dimension and of one's spiritual unity with all. The result and the fruit of all this is infinite love and infinite strength. The Vedanta presents the Atman-Brahman as the unified Experience-Field and as inside all beings and outside as well. It therefore is the all. As proclaimed in a famous hymn of *The Srimad Bhagavatam* [VIII.3:3]:

I take refuge in that Self-existent Being in Whom
is this Universe, from Whom is this universe, by
Whom is this universe, Who Himself is this universe,
and Who is beyond this (differentiated nature) as
also beyond that (undifferentiated nature).

If the whole universe is the product of a self-evolving cause, which Vedanta and modern physical science uphold, then that cause must be present in all its evolutionary products, which then have no reality apart from it. This corollary follows whether that cause is viewed as an intelligent principle—Brahman or Atman—as in Vedanta, or as a non-intelligent background material as in modern science. That one cause must account not only for all the objects of experience, but also for all the *subjects* of experience, and for all experience itself. The solar system in relation to the sun, the food we eat, as much as the human metabolic energy that digests it, the coal we burn and the clothes we wear, are all solar energy in different manifestations.

As remarked by Einstein: "There is no place in this new kind of physics both for the field and matter, for the field is the only reality."[33]

Vedanta upholds also that all evolution presupposes involution. If consciousness appears as a datum in evolution from the cell onward, it must be present in the primordial background material of the universe itself. Vedanta defines evolution as evolution of structure and manifestation of consciousness.

"What is the most evolved notion that man has of this universe?" asks Swami Vivekananda, and proceeds to answer: "It is intelligence, the adjustment of part to part. . . . At the beginning, that intelligence becomes involved, and in the end, that intelligence gets evolved. The sum total of the intelligence displayed in the universe must, therefore, be the involved universal intelligence unfolding itself. This universal intelligence is what we call God. Call it by any name, it is absolutely certain that, in the beginning, there is that infinite cosmic intelligence. This Cosmic intelligence gets involved, and it manifests, evolves itself, until it becomes the perfect person, the Christ-like, the Buddha-like one. Then it goes back to its source. That is why all the scriptures say, 'In Him we live and move and have our being.' That is why all the scriptures preach that we come from God and go back to God. Do not be frightened by the theological terms; if terms frighten you, you are not fit to be philosophers. This cosmic intelligence is what the theologians call God."[34]

Clarifying his use of the word "God," he continues: "I have been asked many times, 'Why do you use that old word 'God'?' Because it is the best word for our purpose. You cannot find a better word than that, because all the hopes, aspirations, and happiness of humanity have been centered in that word. It is impossible now to change that word. Words like these were first coined by great saints who realized their import and understood their meaning. But as they become current in society, ignorant people take these words, and the result is that they lose their spirit and glory. . . .

"Use the old word, only use it in the true spirit, cleanse it of superstition and realise fully what this great ancient word means. If you understand the power of the laws of association, you will know that these words are associated with innumerable majestic and powerful ideas. They have been used and worshipped by millions of human souls, and associated by them with all that is highest and best, all that is rational, all that is lovable, and all that is great and grand in human nature. And they come as suggestions of these associations and cannot be given up. If I tried to express all these by only telling you that God created the universe, it would have conveyed no meaning to you. Yet, after all this struggle, we have come back to Him, the ancient and supreme one."[35]

Brahman-Atman is the unity of all experience. It is the Unified Experience-Field. Differences between the objects, between the object and the subject, and between the subjects themselves, which common sense reveals, and which provide the starting point, and act as the challenge, to knowledge, are overcome in the unity of Brahman-Atman, the non-dual Pure Consciousness, say the *Upanishads*. "Knowledge leads to unity and ignorance to diversity,"[36] said Sri Ramakrishna. All progress of knowledge in science and religion confirms that diversity is on the surface, but deep down is unity. And unity, unlike uniformity, does not eliminate diversity. Knowledge only reveals, but does not add to or take away from, reality. Vedanta therefore proclaims the message of unity in diversity.

Through the positive sciences, we seek for unity in diversity in the world of outer nature, the world of the not-self. This search may be conducted at the purely intellectual level. But when we carry that search into the world of inner nature, the world of the self, the world of consciousness, such an intellectual approach becomes inadequate and misleading. For here we are in the most intimate field of experience, *where all true knowing ever seeks to find its consummation in being*, and where mere intellectual knowledge leaves us far away from our true self. Such self-realization, as it penetrates deeper spiritually, steadily breaks down the barrier between humanity and nature and between one person and another.

THE ATMAN-BRAHMAN OF VEDANTA: ITS IMMENSE SWEEP

Giving a scientific definition of the comprehensive nature of Brahman, or God, or Pure Consciousness, as undertsood in Vedanta, Shankaracharya says in his commentary on the *Taittiriya Upanishad* [III.1]:

> Brahman is defined as that Reality from which beings do not get separated during the time of their origin, maintenance, or dissolution.

It is necessary for us to grasp the immense sweep of the Reality conveyed by the Atman-Brahman of the *Upanishads*. It is far different from the extra-cosmic God of all the monotheistic religions. We get a glimpse of its sweep and range from a passage in Vivekananda's first of two lectures on the *Katha Upanishad* under the title *Realization*, delivered in London in 1896. Though a bit long, it merits reproduction in this context:

> Such a solution of the universal problem as we can get from the outside labours under this difficulty that, in the first place, the universe we see is our own particular universe, our own view of Reality. That Reality we cannot see through the senses; we cannot comprehend It. We only know the universe from the point of view of beings with five senses. Suppose we obtain another sense, the whole universe must change for us. Suppose we had a magnetic sense, it is quite possible that we might then find millions and millions of forces in existence which we do not now know, and for which we have no present sense or feeling. Our senses are limited, very limited indeed; and within these limitations exists that we call our universe; and our God is the solution of that universe; but that cannot be the solution of the whole problem.
>
> But man cannot stop there. He is a thinking being and wants to find a solution which will comprehensively explain all the universes. He wants to see a world which is at once the world of men, and of gods, and of all possible beings, and to find a solution, which will explain all phenomena.
>
> We see, we must find the universe which includes all universes. We must find something which, by itself must be the material running through all these various plans of existence, whether we apprehend it through the senses or not. If we could possible find something which we could know as the common property of the lower as well as the higher worlds, then our problem would be solved. Even if by the sheer force of logic alone we could understand that there must be one basis of all existence, then our problem might approach to some sort of solution. But this solution certainly cannot be obtained only through the world we see and know, because it is only a partial view of the whole.
>
> Our only hope then lies in penetrating deeper. The early thinkers of India discovered that the farther away they were from the center, the more marked were the variations and differentiations, and that the nearer they approached the center, the nearer they were to unity. . . . We, first, therefore, want to find somewhere a center from which, as it were, all the other planes of existence start, and standing there, we should try to find a solution. This is the proposition. And where is that Center? *It is within us*. The ancient sages penetrated deeper and deeper until they

found that, in the innermost core of the human soul, is the center of the whole universe. All the planes gravitate towards that one point. That is the common ground, and standing there alone can we find a common solution.[37] [italics added]

THE ATMAN AS PURE CONSCIOUSNESS: THE LIGHT OF ALL LIGHTS

The Atman as pure and non-dual Consciousness is presented by The *Brhadaranyaka Upanishad* in the following utterance [III.7:23]:

> He is never seen, but is the Seer; He is never heard, but is the Hearer; He is never thought, but is the Thinker; He is never known but is the Knower. There is no other seer but Him, no other hearer but Him, no other thinker but Him, no other knower but Him. He is the *antaryami* (Inner Ruler), your own immortal Self. Everything else but Him is mortal.

The *Upanishads* arrive at the purity, immutability, and non-duality of the Atman and its character as the light of all lights—*jyotisham jyotih*—through a penetrating inquiry into the universal phenomena of the three states of waking, dream, and dreamless sleep. Apart from the two large *Upanishads*, namely, the *Brhadaranyaka* and the *Chandogya*, in which this subject finds prominent treatment, there is one *Upanishad* in which it forms the exclusive theme. This is the *Mandukya*, the shortest of all the *Upanishads* with only twelve verses, whose brief but pregnant utterances have been clarified and amplified by two later sages and philosophers, namely, Gaudapada of the seventh century A.D. in his famous *Mandukyakarika*, and Shankaracharya of the eighth century A.D., in his commentary on the same. The nature of the Atman as pure and non-dual Consciousness revealed by this investigation has been expounded to us in the luminous seventh verse of this *Mandukya Upanishad* [I. 7.]:

> Not conscious of the internal (i.e., the Atman is not exclusively the self in the dream state), nor conscious of the external (the Atman is not exclusively the self in the waking state), nor conscious of both (the self of reverie), not a mass of consciousness (deep sleep), not consciousness, nor unconsciousness, unseen (by the sense organs), beyond the texture of all relativity, incomprehensible (by the sense-bound mind), without any distinguishing mark (therefore beyond logical inference), unthinkable, indescribable, of the essence of the Consciousness of the Unity of the Self, the very cessation of the world of relativity, peaceful, full of bliss and non-dual—this is what is known as the *Turiya* or the Fourth (with respect to the three states). This is the Atman, and it has to be realised.

Introducing this verse, Shankaracharya comments: "Since the *Turiya* or the Atman, being beyond all operations of speech, cannot be brought under the purview of any utterance, the Upanishad desires to describe It by the negation of all attributes."[38]

The *Katha Upanishad* presents the Atman, the Ultimate Reality, as also the intimate Reality, and exhorts individuals to find their peace in this Truth [V.12–13]:

> The one (supreme) Controller of all, the inner Self of all beings, who makes His one form manifold – those *dhiras* (wise men) who realise Him as existing in their own self, to them belongs eternal happiness and to none else.
>
> The Eternal among the non-eternals, the Intelligence among the intelligent, who, though one, fulfills the desires of the many – those *dhiras* who perceive Him as existing within their own self, to them belongs eternal peace and to none else.

Speaking on the Atman in America, Swami Vivekananda said: "No books, no scriptures, no science can ever imagine the glory of the Self that appears as a human being, the most glorious God that ever existed, exists, or ever will exist."[39]

Again, speaking on *The Real and the Apparent Man*, the Swami says: "In worshipping God, we have been always worshipping our own hidden Self."[40]

Describing the Atman as the light of all lights, the light of Pure Consciousness, the *Katha Upanishad* says [V.15]:

> There (in that Atman, in that infinite and non-dual Pure Consciousness), the sun does not illumine, nor the moon and the stars; nor do these lightings illumine (there); and much less this (domestic) fire. When That shines, everything shines after That. By Its light, all this (manifested universe) is lighted.

This light within the heart is not any physical radiation, but the light of Pure Consciousness. It is *adhumakah*, smokeless, free from ignorance, delusion and sorrow. In the words of Patanjali Yoga Sutra, [I.36] – "Or (by meditation on) the effulgent light which is beyond all sorrow." The meditation on the Atman as the light in one's heart is not meant to imprison us in our little selves, but to release us into the light of all lights, the light by which "the whole universe is lighted."

The most persistent search of the human heart is for this light. In the *Gayatri*, the greatest prayer of the Indo-Aryans, one prays for the light of understanding; in another one prays to be redeemed from darkness to light. The perfect one is known as Buddha, the illumined one. The apparently limited light in human beings and the infinite light of God, which kindles the universe, are one and the same, says Vedanta. By penetrating to the light in one's heart, we can reach the light that lights the hearts of all. In the beautiful words of St. John's Gospel [I.9]; "the true Light, which lighteth every man that cometh into the world."

Notes

HUMAN BEING IN DEPTH: SCIENCE AND RELIGION

1. Karl Pearson. Grammar of Science. London: A. and C. Black Ltd., 1900, p. 6.

2. J. Arthur Thomson. Introduction to Science. New York: Holt, Rinehart & Winston, 1934, p. 58.

3. Swami Vivekananda. Complete Works, 9th ed. Calcutta: Advaita Ashrama, vol. 2, p. 433.

4. Swami Vivekananda. Complete Works, 11th ed. Calcutta: Advaita Ashrama, vol. 1, p. 367.

5. Ibid., p367.

6. Swami Vivekananda. Complete Works, 6th ed. Calcutta: Advaita Ashrama, vol. 6, p. 81.

7. Swami Vivekananda. Complete Works, 9th ed. Calcutta: Advaita Ashrama, vol. 2, p. 432.

8. Sir Arthur Eddington. Philosophy of the Physical Science. Cambridge, England: Cambridge University Press, 1939, p. 5.

9. J. Arthur Thompson. Introduction to Science, p. 215.

10. Samuel Coleridge, in J. Arthur Thompson's Introduction to Science, p. 208.

11. Sir Julian Huxley. Evolution after Darwin. Chicago: University of Chicago Press, 1960, p. 17.

12. Eddington. Philosophy of the Physical Sciences, p. 16.

13. Ibid., p. ix.

14. Thomas Huxley. Methods and Results. New York: Appleton-Century-Crofts, 1903. vol. 1, p. 164–65.

15. Willis Harman. "Reconciling Science and Religion" in New Realities. Jan.Feb,1987: p. 55 and 56.

16. Sir James Jeans. The New Background of Science. Cambridge University Press, 1947. p. 68

17. Swami Nityaswarupananda. Astavakra Samhita. 5th ed. (Calcutta: Advaita Ashrama, 1981), p, 29.

18. Lincoln Barnett. The Universe and Dr. Einstein, Mentor ed. (New York: Morrow and Co:, 1949), p. 126–27.

19. Teilhard de Chardin. The Phenomenon of Man, (London: William Collins and Son; New York: Harper and Row, 1959), p. 35–36

20. Ibid., p. 52.

21. Ibid., p. 55

22. Ibid., p. 56.

23. Sir Charles Sherrington. Man on His Nature, Pelican ed. (New York: Cambridge University Press, 1935) p. 38

24. Fred Hoyle. The Intelligent Universe. (New York: Holt, Rinehart & Winston, 1984). p. 202.

25. Renee Weber. Dialogues with Scientists and Sages. (Boston, Mass:, Routledge and Kegan Paul,Ltd., 1986), p. 105, 109, 116–17.

26. Swami Vivekananda. Complete Works. 11th ed., vol.1, p. 15.

27. Sir James Jeans. The New Background of Science. p. 307.

28. Ibid., p. 2–6.

29. Romain Rolland, The Life of Swami Vivekananda. (Calcutta: Advaita Ashrama, 1947), p. 289.

30. Swami Vivekananda, Complete Works. 9thed., vol. 2, p. 40.

31. Sri Krishna. Srimad Bhagavatam. XI. 7: 19–20.

32. Brhadaranyaka Upanishad. III. 4:1.

33. William Grey Walter, The Living Brain. (London: Gerald Duckworth and Co., 1963), p. 16.

34. Ibid., p. 16–17.

35. Ibid., p. 39.

36. Katha Upanishad, VI. 10–11.

37. Huxley, Evolution after Darwin, vol. 3, p. 251–252.

38. Ibid., vol. 3, p. 261–62.

39. Ibid., vol. 1, p. 20.

40. Ibid., vol. 1, p. 21.

41. Grey Walter, The Living Brain, p. 2.

42.. Bertrand Russell, The Impact of Science on Society. (London: Allen and Unwin, 1968), p. 120–21.

43. Grey Walter, The Living Brain, p. 16.

44. Ibid., p. 1, 16.

45. Renee Weber, Dialogues, p. 30.

46. Ibid., p. 30.

47. H. G. Wells and Julian Huxley, The Science of Life. (NY: Doubleday and Doran Co., Inc., 1931). p. 1433, 1434, 1472, 1473.

48. Swami Vivekananda. JnanaYoga. (New York: Ramakrishna-Vivekananda Center, 1945), p. 29–30.

49. Shankaracharya. Srimad Bhagavad Gita Bhashya. (Madras: Ramakrishna Math, 1983), XI.55.

50. Swami Vivekananda, Complete Works. 11th ed., (Calcutta: Advaita Ashrama), vol. 1, p. 6–7.

51. Mundaka Upanishad. I. 1:4.

52. Gospel of Sri Ramakrishna. (New York: Ramakrishna-Vivekananda Center, 1942), p. 524.

53. Mundka Upanishad. I. 1:5.

54. Ibid., III. 1:6

55. Robert Ernest Hume. The Thirteen Principal Upanishads. (New York: Oxford University Press, 1921), p. 30.

56. Katha Upanishad. III. 12.

57. Eight Upanishads wuth commentary of Shankaracharya. (Calcutta: Advaita Ashrama, 1972.) Katha. V.2.

58. Peter Tompkins and Christopher Bird. The Secret Life of Plants. (New York: Harper & Row, 1973.) p. xiv.

59. Ibid., p. 87–88.

60. Ibid., p. 101

61. Ibid., p. 372

62. Shvetasvatara Upanishad. VI.20.

63. Arthur Schopenhauer. Die Welt als Wille and Vorstellung. English trans. (New York: Scribner. 1903.) vol. 1, p. 404.

64. Swami Vivekananda. Complete Works. 8th ed., vol. 4, p. 35.

65. Russell. The Impact of Science on Society. p. 114.

66. Pitirim Sorokin. Reconstruction of Humanity. (Boston: Beacon Press, 1948.) p. 57.

67. Swami Vivekananda. Complete Works. 8th ed., vol. 4, p. 358.

68. Ibid., 8th ed., vol. 3, p. 4.

69. Ibid., 8th ed., vol. 4, p. 155.

70. Russell. Impact of Science on Society, p.77.

71. Sri Shankaracharya. Srimad Bhagavad Gita Bhashya. (Madras: Ramakrishna Math, 1983.) VII. 27–28.

72. Brahma Sutra Bhashya of Shankaracharya. 3ed. (Bombay: Satyàbhamabai Pandurang, 1948.) II.

73. Ibid., IV.

74. Ibid., II.

75. Katha Upanishad. III. 12.

76. George Gaylord Simpson. The Meaning of Evolution. (New Haven, Conn: Yale University Press, 1964.) p. 312.

77. Sri Shankaracharya. Srimad Bhagavad Gita Bhashya. VII: 27–28.

78. Swami Vivekananda. Complete Works. 11th ed. vol. 1, p. 185.

79. Werner Heisenberg. Physics and Philosophy. (New York: Harper and Row, 1962.) p. 197.

80. Ibid., p. 28,29.

81. Mandukya Upanishad. verse 7.

82. Erwin Schroedeinger. What is Life? (New York: Cambridge University Press, 1944) p. 90–91.

83. Sutta Pitaka, Majjhima Nikaya, Sutta 26: Ariya-pariyesana Sutta.

84. Majjhima Nikaya, Sutta 26.

85. Udana, 80–81. Trans. by Frank Lee Woodward. Pali Text Society, 1926.

86. Gaudapada. Manduka Upanishad Karika. III. 33.

87. Ibid., IV. 1

88. Gospel of Sri Ramakrishna. (New York: Ramakrishna-Vivekananda Center, 1942.) p. 524.

89. Brhadaranyaka Upanishad. II.1.20.

90. Swami Vivekananda. Complete Works, 11th ed., vol. 1, p. xiii-xiv.

91. Sir Arthur Eddington. Space, time, and gravitation. (New York: Macmillan, 1920.)

92. Fritjof Capra. The Tao of Physics. Shambala publications, 1975. p. 25.

93. Ibid., p. 25.

94. Ibid., p. 51.

95. Ibid., p. 130–131

96. Ibid., p. 186–187.

97. Ibid., p. 211 .

98. Ibid., p. 300.

99. Ibid., p. 305.

100. Swami Vivekananda. Complete Works. 11th ed., vol. 6, p. 124.

101. Shvetasvatara Upanishad. II:5, III:8.

Notes

FAITH AND REASON IN OUR SCIENTIFIC AGE

1. T. S. Eliot. "The Hollow Men", in *Interpreting Literature,* rev. ed., by K. L. Knickerbocker and H. Willard Reminger. (New York: Holt, Rinehart and Winston, 1960.) p. 403–05. A poem on moral and spiritual decay.

2. Kenneth Scott Latourette. A History of Christianity. (New York: Harper and Row, 1953.) p. 72.

3. Encyclopedia of Religion and Ethics. vol. 5, p. 6.

4. Latourette. A History of Christianity. p. 731.

5. Burton Stevenson. Home Book of Quotations, 9th ed., rev. (New York: Dodd, Mead and Co., 1958.) p. 620.

6. Abraham Maslow. New Knowledge in Human Values. (New York: Harper, 1959.)

7. Carl Jung. The Portable Jung. New York: Penguin, 1976. p. 468.

8. Qadi Sa'd. Studies in the Foreign Relations of India, Professor H. K. Sherwini Felicitation Volume. State Archives of Andhra Pradesh, India. n.d., p. 358–59.

9. Theodor Goldstucker. Panini: His Place in Sanskrit Literature. 1st Indian ed., (India, Chowkhamba, 1965.) p. 95–96.

10. Dr. V. S. Agarwala. India as known to Panini. (Luchnow, Luchnow University, 1953.) p. 2–3.

11. The Anguttara Nikaya, Pali Publication Board, 1960 ed., 1960 ed., Nalanda-Devanagari, Pali Series, vol. I: 3.7.5.

12. Shankaracharya. Vivekachudamani, verse 25.

13. Thompson. Introduction to science. (New York: Holt, 1934.) p. 22.

14. Robert Oppenheimer. Letters and Recollections., ed. by Alice Smith and Charles Weiner. (Boston, Mass: Harvard University Press, 1980.) p. 288.

15. Max Planck. Quantum Questions., ed. by Ken Wilber. (Boston, Mass: New Science Library, 1984.) p. 152.

16. Eddington. Philosophy of Physical Science, p. 222.

17. Albert Einstein. Out of My Later Years. (Secaucus, New Jersey: Citadel Press, 1974.) p. 26.

18. Bergen Evans. Dictionary of Quotations. (New York: Delacorte Press, 1968.) p. 140.

19. Bhagavad Gita. II.49.

20. Srimad Bhagavatam. I: 2. 12.

21. Planck. Quantum Questions. p. 141.

22. Capra. The Tao of Physics. p. 31.

23. Grey Walter. The Living Brain. p. 2.

24. The Gospel of Sri Ramakrishna. (New York: Ramakrishna-Vedanta Center, 1942) p. 802.

25. Chandogya Upanishad. VI. 1: 2–7.

26. Ibid., VI. 12: 1–2.

27. Chandogya Upanishad, with the commentary of Shankaracharya. (Calcutta: Advaita Ashrama, 1983.) VI. 12. 2.

28. Capra. The Tao of Physics, p. 221–23.

29. Brhadaranyaka Upanishad, II. 1:20.

30. Chandogya Upanishad, VI. 12:3.

31. Capra. The Tao of Physics, p. 273.

32. Geoffrey Chew. Great Ideas Today. (Chicago: Encyclopedia Brittanica, 1974.) p. 99.

33. The Gospel of Sri Ramakrishna, p. 398.

34. Ibid., p. 653.

35. Rig Veda, Book 1, Hymn 164, Sloka 46.

36. The Gospel of Sri Ramakrishna, p. 158.

37. Srimad Bhagavatam, I. 2:11.

38. Taittiriya Upanishad, II. 7:1.

39. Bhagavad Gita, XIII. 15–17; 27 and 30.

40. Brahma-Sutra Bhashya. (Calcutta: Advaita Ashrama, 1965.) I. 1. 4.

41. Sir Charles Sherrington. Man on His Nature, p. 266.

42. Sir Arthur Eddington. The Nature of the Physical World. (Cambridge, England: Cambridge University Press, 1928.) p. 281.

43. Drg-Drsya-Viveka. 6th ed., (Mysore, India: Sri Ramakrishna Ashrama, 1976.) versesl, 30.

44. Brhadaranyaka Upanishad with the commentary of Shankaracharya. (Calcutta: Advaita Ashrama, 1975.) 1. 4: 10.

45. Renee Weber. Dialogues. p. 41.

46. Renee Weber and David Bohm. Quantum Implications, ed. by B. J. Hiley, (New York: Routledge, Chapman and Hall, Inc. 1987.) p. 436.

47. Ibid., p. 450.

48. Thomas Huxley, Methods and Results, vo. 1, p. 161 et passim.

49. Capra. The Tao of Physics, p. 306.

50. Gospel of Sri Ramakrishna, p. 729.

51. Ibid., p. 13.

52. Sir Arthur Eddington. Science and the Unseen World. (New York; Macmillan and Co., 1929.) p. 5.

53. Katha Upanishad. IV.1.

54. Mandukya Upanishad. III. 41.

55. Taittiriya Upanishad, II. 9.

56. Mahatma Gandhi. The Story of My Experiments with Truth. (Washington, D. C.: Public Affairs Press, 1948.) p. 4.

57. American Reporter 11 June 1952.

58. Mahabharata. Udyogaparva. 120.

59. Katha Upanishad, VI: 7–9.

60. Swami Vivekananda. Complete Works. 6th ed., vol. 6, p. 56.

61. H. Schipperges, "Aspects of an Upheaval in Medicine" in Electromedica, issue 5, 1970. p. 300.

62. Sherrington. Man on His Nature. p. 266.

63. Eddington. The Nature of the Physical World. p. xvi–xvii.

64. Swami Saradananda. Sri Ramakrishna, the Great Master. 5th rev. ed., (Madras: Sri Ramakrishna Math, 1979.) p. 893.

65. Buddha. The Dhammapada., ed. by Sarvapali Radhakrishnan. New York: Oxford University Press, 1950.) p. 11.

66. Brahma-Sutra Bhashya. Sutras 1–4.

67. Sarvapali Radhakrishnan. Indian Philosophy. (London: Allen and Unwin, 1929, 1940.) vol. 1, p. 143.

Notes

HUMAN BEING IN DEPTH: CONSCIOUSNESS ITSELF

1. John White, ed. The Highest State of Consciousness. (New York: Doubleday and Co., Inc., Anchor Books, 1972.) p. ix.

2. Ibid., p. 471.

3. Daniel Goleman and Richard Davidson, eds. Consciousness: the Brain, States of Awareness and Alternate Realities. (New York: Harper and Row, Inc. 1979.) p. 192–94.

4. Robert E. Ornstein, ed. The Nature of Human Consciousness. (New York: W. H. Freeman, 1968.) p. 5.

5. Ibid., p. 41.

6. Swami Akhilananda: Mental Health and Hindu Psychology; Hans Jacobs: Western Psychotherapy and Hindu Sadhana; Geraldine Coster: Yoga and Western Psychology; Erich Fromm et al: Zen Buddhism and Psychoanalysis; Newsweek, Nov. 7, 1988 "Body and Soul", p. 90; John Welwood, ed.: The Meeting of the Ways: Explorations in East/West Psychology.

7. Richard Davenport. An Outline of Animal Development. (Reading, Mass: Addison-Wesley, 1979.) p. 242–250.

8. Ibid., p. 390.

9. Ibid., p. 402–403.

10. Sri Shankaracharya. Srimad Bhagavad Gita Bhashya. (Madras: Ramakrishna Math, 1983.) 7.6.

11. Erich Jantsch. Evolution and Consciousness. (Reading, Mass. Addison-Wesley, 1976.) p. 230–231.

12. Capra. The Tao of Physics. p. 211.

13. Swami Vivekananda. The Complete Works. vol. 5, p. 253.

14. Katha Upanishad, 3: 3–9.

15. Bhagavad Gita, 6:21.

16. Grey Walter. The Living Brain. p. 16.

17. Erich Jantsch. The Self-Organizing Universe. (Oxford, England: Pergamon, 1979, p. 19.

18. Chandogya Upanishad, 6. 8:7.

19. Swami Vivekananda. Complete Works, vol. 3, p. 330–331.

20. Max Muller. Three lectures on the Vedanta Philosophy. (London: Longmans Green and Co., 1894.) p. 7.

21. Eight Upanishads with the Commentary of Shankaracharya. (Calcutta: Advaita Ashrama, 1972.) Katha. III. 10.

22. Katha Upanishad. III. 10–11.

23. Sarvapali Rakhakrishnan, The Bhagavad Gita. (London: Allen and Unwin, 1948.) p. 177.

24. Shankaracharya. Vivekachudamani, 125. 126.

25. Katha Upanishad. III. 12.

26. Eight Upanishads with the Commentary of Shankaracharya. Katha. III. 12.

27. Katha Upanishad. III. 13.

28. Eight Upanishads with the Commentary of Shankaracharya. Katha. III. 15.

29. J. G. Jennings. The Vedantic Buddhism of the Buddha. (London: Oxford University Press, 1947.) p. 40.

30. Swami Saradananda. Sri Ramakrishna, the Great Master. 5th rev. ed., (Madras: Sri Ramakrishna Math, 1978.) vol. 1, p. 417–418.

31. The Gospel of Sri Ramakrishna, p. 243.

32. Bhagavad Gita. Trans. by Swami Prabhavananda. (New York: Harper and Row, n. d.) Chapter 2, verses 1–4; 13–14.

33. M. Capek. The Philosophical Impact of Contemporary Physics. Van Nostrand, 1961.)

34. Swami Vivekananda. Complete Works, 9th ed., vol. 2, p. 209–210.

35. Ibid., p. 210.

36. Sri Ramakrishna's Teachings. Part II. (Calcutta: Advaita Ashrama, 1920.) p. 53.

37. Swami Vivekananda. Complete Works. 9th ed., vol. 2, p. 156.

38. Shankaracharya. Ten Principal Upanishads. Mandukya Upanishad. (Delhi: Motilal Banarsidass, 1964.) VII.

39. Swami Vivekananda. Complete Works. 9th ed., vol. 2, p. 250.

40. Ibid., p. 279.

Glossary

Advaita Non-dualistic Vedanta

Amrta Spirituality of the mystic dimension; immortality

Ashtavakra Samhita A short treatise on non-dualistic Vedanta from the time of the *Upanishads*

Atman The divine within the person

Bhagavad Gita One of the three main scriptures within Vedanta

Bhagavan The All-loving personal aspect of Brahman or God

Bhagavatam A famous devotional scripture with stories of ancient seers and kings, including some of Sri Krishna's life

Brahma-Sutras A treatise dealing with the knowledge of Brahman in the form of aphorisms

Bhakti Love of God

Bodhi Spiritual enlightenment

Buddhi Enlightened reason; discriminative faculty

Cit Consciousness as an aspect of Brahman

Dama Discipline of the sense organs

Dharma Social ethics and personal morality

Dhiras Heroes; wise one

Drshyam Precepts and concepts

Gaudapada (before eighth century A.D.) Vedantic philosopher and exponent of non-dualism

Jinnasa Inquiry

Jnanam Spiritual knowledge

Kosha Sheath; a covering – the Atman or Self is covered by five sheaths

Krishna (ca. 1500 B.C.) Regarded as an Incarnation of God by the Hindus. His birth date precedes that of Buddha by one-thousand years approximately.

Kundalini The spiritual energy dormant in human beings. Manifests itself in mystic experiences and different degrees of illumination.

Loka Sensory world; a plane of existence

Lokottara Trans-sensory; transcendental plane of existence

Manas Mind; sometimes translated as incipient mind

Mantra A short prayer; a name of God to be repeated, representing an aspect of God

Maya Relative changing existence; the power of Brahman, from which it is eternally inseparable

Moksha Freedom as liberation from all worldly bondage

Nirvikalpa A supreme state of consciousness, transcendental of a non-dualistic nature

Om The Logos; a sacred syllable representing both the Impersonal and Personal aspect of the Absolute

Parak rupa The without of nature

Paramatman The Supreme Self; supreme Atman

Pradhana Basic material out of which all objects have come; nature

Prajna Wisdom

Prakrti Nature primordial; the material of the universe

Pratyak rupa Within of nature

Purusha The Self; the Atman in Vedanta philosophy

Rajas The active principle; energetic state

Ramakrishna (1836–1886) A God man of the highest and unique spiritual attainment, who after practicing various modes or worship, taught that as many religions so many paths to God or the Ultimate Reality, provided the seeker was earnest and sincere. He inspired the modern renaissance of Vedanta and is considered a world teacher. A group of unusual aspirants became his disciples and his message of the harmony of religions has spread over the globe.

Sadhana Spiritual practice

Shakti Energy or power within nature; dynamic aspect of the Godhead

Samsara Worldliness; the cycle of birth, death and rebirth

Samyak Jnana Comprehensive and perfect knowledge of total Reality

Samskara Impression that has been created in the mind

Sat Existence Absolute; pure Being

Sattva The pure, fine and calm state of being and energy

Shama Discipline of the mind

Shankaracharya (*a.d.* 788–820) One of the greatest philosopher saints of India. He died at the age of 32. He organized monastic systems that still exist in India. Wrote many commentaries on the *Brahma-Sutras, Gita,* and *Upanishads.* Authored the *Crest Jewel of Discrimination,* a classic non-dualistic text.

Shraddha Faith

Shruti Eternal religion; perennial philosophy as in the *Upanishads*

Smriti Local; parochial, but also traditional law, secular as well as religious

Tamas Inert state of energy; stupidity; sloth

Susupti State of deep sleep

Triputi The triple group of knowledge, the knower, and the object of knowledge

Turiya Transcendental; superconsciousness

Vasana Impressions left in the mind by past thoughts and actions

Vijnana Enlightened reason

Vivekananda (1863–1902) a monastic disciple and chief apostle of Sri Ramakrishna. Represented Vedanta at World's Parliament of Religions in Chicago in 1893 and later lectured throughout the U.S. and in London. Founded the Ramakrishna Mission in India. He was a saint of the highest order dedicated to the worship of God in every being.

Yuga dharma The ethics of a particular era

Bibliography

Astavakra Samhita. 5th ed. Calcutta: Advaita Ashrama, 1981.

Barnett, Lincoln. The Universe and Dr. Einstein. New York: William Morrow and Co., Mentor, 1949.

The Bhagavad Gita. Trans. by Swami Prabhavananda. New York: Harper and Row Publishers, n.d.

The Bhagavad Gita. Calcutta: Advaita Ashrama, n.d. various editions

Brahma-Sutra Bhashya of Shankaracharya. Trans by Swami Gambhirananda. Calcutta: Advaita Ashrama, 1965.

Brhadaranyaka Upanishad. Madras: Sri Ramakrishna Math, 1945.

Capek, M. The Philosophical Impact of Contemporary Physics. New York: Van Nostrand, 1961.

Capra, Fritjof. The Tao of Physics. Boston: Shambala publications, 1975.

———. The Turning Point. New York: Simon and Schuster, 1982.

Eddington, Sir Arthur. Philosophy of Physical Science. London: Cambridge University Press, 1939.

Einstein, Albert. Out of My Later Years. Secaucus, NJ: Citadel Press, 1974.

Eight Upanishads. Trans. by Swami Gambhirananda with commentary of Shankaracharya. 2 vols. Calcutta: Advaita Ashrama, 1972.

Goleman, Daniel and Richard Davidson, ed. Consciousness; the Brain, States of Awareness and Alternate Realities. New York: Harper and Row Publishers, 1979.

The Gospel of Sri Ramakrishna. New York: Ramakrishna-Vivekananda Center, 1942.

Grey Walter, William. The Living Brain. London: Gerald Duckworth, 1963.

Heisenberg, Werner. Physics and Philosophy. New York: Harper and Row Publishers, 1962.

Hiley, B. J., ed. Quantum Implications. New York: Routledge, Chapman and Hall, Inc., 1987.

Hoyle, Fred. The Intelligent Universe. New York: Holt, 1984.

Huxley, Sir Julian. Evolution After Darwin. Chicago: University of Chicago Press, 1960.

Jantsch, Erich. Evolution and Consciousness. Reading, Mass: Addison-Wesley, 1976.

Jantsch, Erich. The Self-organizing Universe. Oxford, England: Pergamon, 1979.

Russell, Bertrand. The Impact of Science on Society. London: Allen & Unwin, 1952.

Saradananda, Swami. Ramakrishna, the Great Master. Madras; Sri Ramakrishna Math, 1978.

Sheldrake, Rupert. A New Science of Life. Los Angeles: J. P. Tarcher, Inc., 1981.

Sherrington, Sir Charles. Man on His Nature. Pelican ed., New York: Cambridge University Press, 1935.

Simpson, George C. The meaning of Evolution. New Haven, Conn: Yale University Press, 1964.

Vivekananda, Swami. Complete Works. 8 vols. Calcutta: Advaita Ashrama. various dates.

Wilber, Ken, ed. Quantum Questions. Boston, Mass: New Science Library, 1984.

Index